Funny Stories Good Luck Bad Luck

Manish Sharma

Published by Manish Sharma, 2023.

While every precaution has been taken in the preparation of this book, the publisher assumes no responsibility for errors or omissions, or for damages resulting from the use of the information contained herein.

Funny Stories Good Luck Bad Luck

Life is full of many ups and down, which consists of good and bad learning experiences

By Manish Sharma

My Life mantra: Spread the sea of knowledge and raise the bar of wisdom globally.

To almighty god, to whom I shall always remain grateful for providing me this inspirational opportunity to write this book based on various life experiences, which I feel were amusing moments with a combination of good and bad luck.

Preface

First edition

Many peoples have written autobiographies and shared every tiny detail of their Life that may be more or less a confession or life struggle before reaching success.

This book is not about any confession or Life struggle but a journey of a beautiful life on a curved mountain and valley, having many unforgettable funny moments of ups and down with a mixed bunch of happiness and sadness.

You will enjoy reading this book right from the first page till the end and find yourself in many situations with a broad priceless smile.

I will say oh yes! It's me.

Let us live our Life reading through this book.

Why This Book?

Everyone on this earth has gone through various phases of Life, right from their childhood to their final destiny.

This journey of Life brought them many bitter and sweeter experiences; those with a passage of time in the later stage of Life seem to be of amusing moments, and you started laughing at yourself.

It is a tragedy that bitter experience is always more frequent than sweeter experience and always teaches us a lesson.

Each one of us feels great when we remember old memories of Life and would like to live past life time and again. It is just like a beautiful dream you have seen once and wanted to recur.

This book is all about those small funny life events where every moment was so powerful to change your final destiny, and you were unaware of this or did not realize it. It is a combination of science, management principles, spirituality, emotions, morality, and social science explained funnily.

It is sure that you can't decide your destiny as per your will or wish; surrounding circumstances at that time determine your life path, and you have only to follow them.

The situation at that time may encourage or discourage you, but later, you will realize that was the only best possible way.

This book is a collection of small funny stories, and each one of you will enjoy reading this book till the last page.

Acknowledgment

Every completed task is the consolidated effort of many peoples; this book is the best example.

I am thankful to my lovely wife and sons for supporting me throughout writing this book.

I am also thankful to all the people who came across me during this fantastic journey and gave me many valuable life lessons that are part of this book.

Since sources were not readily available for the acknowledgment of many peoples, I would be grateful to everyone to be part of this journey for their direct or indirect support to make this task possible.

I am also thankful to those unknown friends and would like to give credit for using sketches as a representation in this book.

If any credit missed to be given inadvertently in the next version, it would be taken care of if brought to the Author's notice.

Chapter 1
Near the Wall> A Adventure With Life or No Life

"You can drink from all sorts of wells, but unless your water source is the Living Water Himself, you will never be satisfied."

Beth Moore

Near the well: Image for representation only

From where should I start? The answer is a trillion-dollar question, which is also very tricky and complex.

We always look for complex answers to complex questions, but often, it surprisingly comes out to be a straightforward answer.

Before the start of this journey, I would like to introduce my two best friends, Good Luck and Bad Luck.

If you are a watcher of the Tom and Jerry cartoon network series, you will find that there is either a win-win or lost-lost situation for both, but they are good friends.

It is altogether a very funny tussle between them for supremacy. It is a see-saw game of entertainment.

Both my friends are also similar, they have never been in a single side of mine.

They are always to find an opportunity to create happiness & sadness respectively in my Life.

It was hardly any incident when they supported me as a team, this fight will continue till the last breath of my life cycle.

You would enjoy the game of chess of check and mate throughout this book; let us start from early childhood.

It is the golden period of Life when you are free from all anxieties and only care that someone should care about you, nothing else, no compromise; this is the only Life's essential highest priority at that time rest is enjoy, enjoy, and enjoy.

Every child is unique, born with ample curiosity, and wants to explore and learn this new world.

Still, the problem is that they want to get all the information as early as possible, keep themselves updated, and would like to evaluate whether Life is rocket science or the reinvention of a wheel again. In the current corporate world, it is mandatory for everyone.

Everyone should be curious so was me; I can't say that I was a few years old because I had celebrated my first birthday only and waited for the second, but it was not me because I didn't know the meaning of a birthday, but it had the purpose to my parent.

It was my first adventure with Life or no life. I can't say it is an experience; at that time, I also didn't know the meaning of experience.

I was staying with my family in the government police quarter happily. My father was a very disciplined and strict policeman.

Those days the only source of all-purpose use water was a deep well, and you had to draw water from a deep well with a bucket tied to a rope made of coconut fiber.

Many a time, I did observe this regular activity. My parent used to do it regularly, and I often went with them.

It raised a lot of curiosity in my mind, and I wanted to satisfy myself with specific answers.

A lovely day, although in those days every day was good for me, that day was exceptionally extraordinary to me as I was alone on my first adventurous trip that goes towards the beautifully designed well, it was the center of attraction as well as the center of gossip of my parents and neighbors also.

In the afternoon, everyone was looking to have a small nap to get rid of tiredness due to the lengthy first half session of the day.

It was a daily activity for everyone, and it was a really boredom time for me, and I was fad-up with this because no one was there to take care of me during that period.

As per routine, my father was in the office, and my mother was, as usual, on the tour of daydreaming; I am sorry; I mean, she was taking a regular noon nap that never lasted a minimum of two hours.

It was the right time for me to go out for my first adventure trip as I started standing on my own feet, nowadays when a young man, when after completing his graduation, starts their professional career, they are now standing on own feet, it was the litmus test for me to see the world as a lonely tourist who will travel to that dream well.

I slowly started moving towards my dream target without knowing whether anyone was watching me because I was not a thief who was afraid of the world and tried to hide. I was an innocent, pure soul.

My dream target was around a hundred meters away from my house; nowadays, in modern corporate language, we call our dream target a "SMART" target that is Specific, Measurable, Attainable, Realistic, and Timely.

For me, everything was in a "SMART" order; it should take a minimum of five minutes to reach there. I'd strictly followed the SMART technique, and all five (i.e., S, M, A, R, & T) were in my favor.

The journey started; slowly-slowly, I was reaching my target. Could you imagine your level of happiness and excitement when you are on a similar trip?

Please feel that excitement right now with one of your experiences; it is fantastic. Finally, I reached there.

Can you imagine the ocean of happiness inside me?

It was not the end; a climax was about to come that was sensational.

As soon as I reached the well, one of our neighbors, a close friend of my mother, saw me standing alone beside the well and trying to look under the well.

For me, this was the topmost adventurous moment as the first time I was alone measuring the depth of the well in my tiny

Life. Well was almost full of water; anyone could see their face clearly in the clean potable water. I started the same.

My replica appeared on a beautiful water canvas.

It was like a colored water portrait of mine, along with a beautiful colored sky in the background.

I was highly excited to see my twin brother. I'd said hello to him, and he replied instantly to me in the same manner as I did.

We were talking to each other pleasantly.

I missed mentioning that my nickname is "Bunty" Please don't link this with Bun and Tea. I am just joking.

In the meantime, my mother's friend woke her up and told her that I was near the well and leaning inside; she got shocked; she was in a deep sleep and perhaps dreaming about innocent lovely Bunty.

She ran immediately towards the house's main door and saw me leaning inside the well and speaking to someone, but it was no other than me. I was talking about my moving, fascinating water image.

There was no immediate contingency action plan available to anyone because my chest was touching the top portion of a wall, like a see-saw; any imbalance in the weight distribution could lead me to fall inside the deep well around a hundred feet depth.

I was enjoying this moment without fear of any unfortunate incident that may lead to fatal.

Many times both my legs left the ground and floated in the air, but as per scientific law, due to the center of gravity being on the lower side of my body, I remained on the external side of the well.

There was a see-saw battle between Life and death.

Outside the well was good luck, who was pulling my leg and trying to keep on the ground endlessly, and on the other side was bad luck, but he was not much interested in ending the game of Life in the beginning.

He was just like a helpless opposition party showing his presence only rather than creating naughtiness.

My mother was about to cry to divert my attention; immediately, her friend stopped her and signaled her to keep quiet and maintain the silence.

There was a pin-drop silence for a moment, and the person passing nearby became a standstill like a statue with no physical movement, just like children used to play statue games regularly with each other.

One person started inching slowly towards me because, with a minor change in my attention, the results could be anything; no one knows.

Time was very short, his pace of movement towards me was languid, and at the same time, my mother's heartbeats were going up and up; no one knew how much it was, maybe 150~200 beats/ minute; you can't measure only imagine, heart was pumping out of the body.

That daring person, I do not know his name, finally, in seven to eight minutes, he reached to me, leaned himself below me because even a slight feeling of presence this person could harm me.

That was the highest stress level with all excitement and the highest level of anxiety; my mother's and nearby people's heartbeats were very high as this was the climax.

That man suddenly gripped my swinging legs and pulled them to the ground, and finally, in the end, he saved me from any untoward incident.

I won my first battle of Life

Life won, and the other side of the Life after Life lost.

Happiness scored over sadness.

Immediately, my mother, who was then only 28 years old at that time, ran at the fastest speed of her time, and at that time, she could beat any international woman sprint runner in 100 meters' race in any international tournament; it didn't matter if it's the Olympics.

My mother filled me in her lap with tears in her eyes and started loving me a lot.

It is the beauty of the universe-proven relationship between mother and child.

Innocent Bunty was the talk of the town, and everybody was showering love on me.

That was my first interaction with god, who was smiling through my face, and there was a celebration of victory.

My mother, my later age, told this story many times to me on different occasions.

The Moral of a Story

"Belief in the superpower of the almighty god, no one can change your destiny without his will, and today, I am humbled to the god to write this story for you."

Chapter 2

Childhood Adventure > Walk on the Highway

"As a child, one has that magical capacity to move among the many eras of the earth; to see the land as an animal does; to experience the sky from the perspective of a flower or a bee; to feel the earth quiver and breathe beneath us; to know a hundred different smells of mud and listen unselfconsciously to the soughing of the trees."

Valerie Andrews, Writer

Courtesy: Walking on a highway: Image for representation only

Childhood is full of curiosity. Most of the experiments with Life happen during this period only.

We want to learn new things through the DIY (Do It Yourself) technique. It is a proven tool to verify and validate any new concept.

It might be a new concept, but being used for years by every child across the globe and satisfied the query raised, the same was happening with me.

You can imagine that we have been using this tool since our childhood without knowing the accuracy of this tool.

I was just shifted with my family to a new location due to my father's job transfer. My father's transfer was a regular activity every three to four years.

It was a wonderful city. My house was in the center, the primary market, and the main road. I was living in a beautiful location.

All the time, there was a good gathering of people from morning till late night.

I was a three years old very cute boy with chubby cheeks and curly hair, and I was very fair as well as was mother's pet, not only mother's pet but also every pet of our neighbors, it was me.

You were thinking that I am rewriting a famous poem, but my friend, it is true, I was like that. I rarely used to stay at home; all the time, I was busy with many of my mother's and father's friends.

It was a big challenge for me to please everyone and maintain a higher energy level to remain energetic till late evening.

The outside world attracts this habit too much.

In the competitive world, maintaining a consistently higher energy level is a big task that I am doing.

When hundreds of people roaming around you and when you are moving here and there with someone, you always try to explore every opportunity to wander alone rather than all the time dependent on others.

Many a time, I'd tried to cross the border but couldn't succeed.

You can control water inside the lake by building the bank around there, but when heavy rain this water mixed in the river, the Silent River becomes turbulent and creates havoc.

The same kind of thunder was taking a violent shape within me; it was waiting for the right opportunity to come out and wipe away the surroundings that no one could stop.

On a very sunny day, I was, as usual, ready with a clean cloth. Fortunately, that day, no one was there to pick me up, my mother was busy with routine tasks with my elder and younger siblings, and my father already went his office.

Today no one was there for me. The tiny toddler was alone in my daily routine Life. I had yet to book a ride with them today.

It was a golden opportunity for me. I'd cautiously inspected the situation, whether I was on the radar of someone or not.

The signal was green, as no one was paying attention to me since they were busy with their daily routine.

The time had come, the first time I'd stepped out of my house alone and entered the world of suspense, curiosity, joy, challenge, opportunity, and threat.

In the business, we regularly do SWOT analysis to find out our Strengths, Weaknesses, Opportunities, and Threats to become successful.

I was also a complete package of all these things at age three.

The road in front of my house directly connects with the country's major highway, where hundreds of big heavy, medium, and light vehicles pass every day.

It is the most significant highway in the country, more than fifteen hundred kilometers in length.

You can't expect such a child to obey the traffic rules.

The distance from my house to the highway was less than half a kilometer.

I do not remember, but along the road, slowly, I reached the main highway.

No one traced me. Now it was the climax!!!

I'd entered a highway, it was a fantastic experience for me, and I'd never seen so many vehicles in such an abundance. After the first journey to the well long back, I was highly excited for this second adventurous journey.

It was my day. Democracy gives you freedom, for example, the right to education, the right to speech, the right to live, and the right to travel across the country.

I may be the youngest pedestrian traveler in the country or the world.

I can't imagine or remember what was going on in my mind, but I was exploring the new world with every new step away from home.

Around the road were gardens, water, trees, birds, and so many exciting things to watch.

I didn't know how much I had explored.

Just like to add one more thing here, due to my father's frequent job location changes, my family shifted again to the same house when I was 13 years old.

Can you imagine the same house, same road, and same highway but not the same people, now that you are at sufficient maturity level and remembering this outing?

Even now, after half a century of age, when I pass through this road, I always have a big smile, and I thought about how it was possible.

Ok.

It might be a kilometer or two distance I'd covered on the highway, but surprisingly, no one paid attention to me.

In the world, if a small cute child is walking abnormally, even a stranger is surprised and checks for his lone traveling due to fear of accident.

Maybe god with me, who was taking care of his creatures by deputing hidden guards, my good luck beside me.

As I always say, Life is beautiful; when everything goes in your way, could you think it would be so easy and smooth?

No, it can't be.

My adventure was about to end, and suddenly, one of our neighbors tracked me, who used to take me for my routine outing.

He couldn't believe that it was me. He shouted at me with my name. He was scared about how it was possible that alone I was there and no one was accompanying him.

I identified him immediately; we used to call him "Mamu." I loudly cried Mamuuuuuuuuuuu.

He ran towards me like a hundred-meter marathon sprinter and tightly grabbed me.

Both were silent and answerless.

He carried me to my house, enquired with my mother, full of anger, and narrated the whole story to her.

There was a shocking surprise on my mother's face; she couldn't believe this miracle could happen.

I miraculously survived any big life-threatening event.

Rest, I did not remember what happened to me, but it was clear that I had more restrictions.

I was in full custody. Not a single bird can touch me without my mother's permission.

It was a delightful ending to my second adventurous journey.

Such an incident might create shivering in everyone, but I was emotionless because I didn't know what emotion was.

The Moral of a Story

"A child has abundant energy, emotion, curiosity, excitement, talent, and creativity. You have to explore right from the beginning and engage them to use their full potential because you never know what miracles he will do later in his Life."

Chapter 3

Class Bunk > Smarter than Teacher

"Sometimes, it's better to bunk a class and enjoy with your friends because now, when I look back, marks never make me laugh, but memories do."

APJ Abdul Kalam, Scientist and Ex-President of India

Courtesy: Class bunk: Image for representation only

Every parent dreams that their child does academic excellence during their education and brings pride to them.

My father had a similar dream for me. Apart from my school studies, he also selected the best teacher in the town for me.

If you compared with current coaching facilities readily available for students, earlier was not the case, options were limited, and you had to perform excellence with those respected teachers only. In those days, along with teaching, personal interaction with the teacher was at the highest level.

In Indian culture, there has been a teacher-student tradition for centuries, where parent hands over their child to the teacher to give them the best of all life's essential lessons and academic knowledge.

A child of ten years of age always looks at life with a lot of fun differently, would like to have a minor education, but love to spend most of the time with friends playing Football, Cricket, making paper boat, and floating in the water, making mud dam in the rainy water, flying kites, taking care of stray dogs, running behind butterfly in the day and firefly in the night, collecting dry tree branches & leaves, and sitting around a wood fire, daily news briefing, storytelling around there, and many more games.

It was entertaining, no doubt about this, and I was not different from them.

In totality, there was no need for any dressing sense in those days as school dress was the same as a social or informal house dress; all were only one.

We have no excuse for our parents for the same we enjoyed this.

Sometimes there was no need to change the dress for three to four days as there was no hygiene or cleanliness concept.

We were happy with dirty clothes, and no one was asking to change the same.

Nowadays, could you believe this? Never. Life was beautiful even after we had either no or limited resources.

We were delighted with our life.

In the evening, praying at the temple was a mandatory part of our childhood to have some spirituality.

All over the world, prayer is a common practice.

But my father had a different plan for me. He not only hired the best teacher in the town but, along with this, sent me to an old Indian language, i.e., Sanskrit school. All the holy books are in this language.

Sanskrit is the world's oldest language. He wanted me to be a priest and a great scholar.

It was a double shock to me; if I had done this, I would not be able to find sufficient time to play and spend quality playtime with my best friends.

Both my friends, good luck and bad luck, were unprepared for this new change because they were also naughty children like me and were enjoying life without ill intentions.

All my other best friends had no burden with these additional studies; they enjoyed every moment of life, even during school.

Circumstances were not in my hand; anyhow, forcefully, I had been asked to attend all three sessions. I tried to manage the show, and from there, my multitasking capability along with time management skills got built up, which is now, in the corporate world, the essential requirement to reach the top of the ladder of success.

During the first four to five months, I learned the tricks of management and did my task with utmost honesty; later on, I realized that my childhood freedom was getting compromised with my future life plan that my parent set.

That was unacceptable to me as a young, growing, independent child.

Democracy had given me all rights to me to live my free life.

I'd started feeling that I was becoming the victim of circumstances; now, it was the right time to become the master of events.

It is another success mantra for everyone that you can be successful only when you overcome the circumstances rather than falling into the net of the vicious circle of events.

I felt that this additional qualification would no longer help me; at the same time, I'd started feeling that I was an extraordinary person with god gifted talent as I was the premium class student in my school as well as in other classes that I had joined there, as my all teachers were giving special attention to me after all I was school topper of my last class.

I started thinking differently to get rid of this tedious additional routine activity.

I had no problem with my regular schooling because I was enjoying the company of all my good friends in school, and we had a perfect time there.

I'd studied the pattern of teaching being followed by my teachers because after returning home, I had to update my mother about the same-day lessons to update my disciplined father, who had a lot of hope for me.

I drafted a strategy and understood the pros and cons of success and failure.

There was every chance anyone would catch hold of me in that small town, which hardly had a population of ten thousand.

Even after forty years, the town's population is the same, possibly due to the population growth level being the same as the migration level.

I'd started my experimental journey now; I'd spend three hours between 2 to 5 pm daily and reached home safely without anyone's doubt.

Initial two hours, I used to spend my journey for entertainment, playing with friends outside the red zone inner circle of my house in a safe area.

I'd utilized the time to watch live cricket and football matches with my best friend; in those days, there was no television; this was the only source of live sports watching.

It was a wonderful life experience that I can't forget. I was on a seventh sky, as no one could track me. There was no mobile or advanced GPS at that time.

Last hour, that was the real smartness that helped me in my later stage of life to develop time management skills, which I am utilizing with ease and effectiveness to date.

In the last hour, that is between 4 to 5 pm. I used to write all the lessons and assignments my teachers gave.

Every day I used to create new versions of projects without a single repetition and showed them to my mother with complete confidence, exactly matching what my teacher used to teach me.

I'd started feeling good and very lucky, my strategy worked very well, and I could execute the task according to plan. Today this is the need of any business.

You can taste success only when you work according to plan; I'd learned another management mantra: if your planning is excellent, you have finished half of the work.

This strategy ran successfully, and I could continue for over a month.

During this period, no one noticed me, even my teacher too. I was not a healthy boy, so my regular illness also helped me to remain safe from teachers' eyes as I regularly remained absent from class in the past due to valid health reasons, and my teacher was aware of this fact.

I'd also carry my tuition fees from my mother to pay my teacher, but it remained with me in my school bag.

But you know that everyone is not perfect in this universe except god. As per *Vince Lombardi, Perfection is not attainable, but if we chase perfection, we can catch excellence.*

My good luck did not last for a longer time. My PDCA cycle (Plan, Do, Check, and Act) was not up to the mark; I'd followed only two steps, Plan and Do but missed the last two steps, which are Check and Act.

To perfect your task, you should have a master of PDCA.

I could not realize that a big storm was about to come in my life and that I would have to face the most significant challenge at the age ten.

One fine day, although that time every day was acceptable to me because I was enjoying this freedom for more than a month, that was not my day; it was, in fact, my family's day.

My additional class teacher's house was at the corner of the triangle roadside; from their three road passes, you may call it TEE POINT.

One road goes towards my house, at another roadside entrance gate was there, and the last one was my favorite route during this tenure; on this route, no one was there who could have recognized me.

It was a completely safe, less populated, and low-traffic route.

My misfortune was already present when I returned home to that corner. I did not realize this earlier due to my fun-involved life phase; when you are in love with your favorite task, you forget everything.

As soon as I reached to corner, I found that my eldest brother was standing there, he immediately noticed, and as I approached him, he immediately asked me about my change in route.

I was shocked by this kind of unexpected encounter. It was just like a natural calamity in my sweet dreams that I was living for many days.

I was immediately answerless but soon recovered, used the presence of mind, and offered a valid reason to him.

I told him at the corner, one wheat flour shop person was singing a beautiful song, and I liked it very much and so to hear that song, so I turned there as the shop was at the corner of my favorite route.

Now, that was a hilarious reason I had given to my brother, who did not buy my idea of change in the route.

He immediately scolded me and produced me in the family Marshall Court before our parents. It was a tough day; this time, I was not an innocent child but faced treatment like a criminal for my criminal offense.

I had been punished heavily by my parent, I can't tell the type and level of punishment I'd received from them, but you can imagine this very well.

They carried me to my teacher, but he refused to continue me as his student after hearing the story. It was a big shock to everyone, as I told you earlier he was the best teacher in the town.

My parent apologized to him repeatedly and asked him to do whatever he could with me; he had complete authority.

My great and kind teacher accepted me once again.

Now good fortune vanished, and bad luck started. Once again, I was the victim of circumstances and accepted the reality.

It has changed my life 360 degrees; the new challenge before me was to perform with perfection.

When my fourth standard examination result was declared, I was on a summer vacation leave at my maternal grandfather's house. I'd scored 90 %, marks highest ever in the school's history in the town.

My father received the mark sheet from my teacher with tears in his eyes.

There were tears in all my family member's eyes too.

Every family member celebrated my success, but for me, I was so shy and felt shame for my act that I could not have the courage to meet my teacher once again; I was the luckiest person to get such a kind of teacher who turnaround my whole life.

Unfortunately, I could not get the opportunity to meet him again; only once, when I finished my technical graduation as a Chemical Engineer, I went to his house, but to my surprise, he had left for his final journey a couple of months before I reached there.

I was his first student who had done engineering; in those days, it was the dream of every small-downtown student and parent.

Tears were in my eyes; I felt unlucky and moved away from his house with a broken heart.

There was a surprise still to come into my life. After moving a few yards from his house, I found my second-best teacher standing before me. I'd fallen on his legs but this time with complete joy.

I told my success story to him; he was so excited to learn about me, as I was his only student who became an engineer during that period.

He held my hand firmly with so much excitement that I had never felt such excitement in my later stage of life; I felt so proud of him and myself.

On the same day, god had shown me two phases of life, that is, sadness and the next one, happiness, which are the two extreme ends of life.

The Moral of a Story

"Good times and tough times never last long, but tough people last long. I learned a lifetime lesson that you should never give up."

Chapter 4

Leave the Home @11 > Fad up of Life

"Whether moving out of state or to a completely different country, moving away from home takes bravery and even more emotional preparation than practical planning – especially if dealing with unsupportive loved ones."

*Brooke Baum, **Moving Away: the Emotional Side of Leaving**[1]*

Leave home: Image for representation only.

Life is full of drama; you must play different roles at different times.

Challenges start as soon as you are born.

These challenges are for survival from the adversity of life that you have to face in every stage of life.

---

1.   https://www.goodreads.com/work/quotes/85961681

Your journey is full of ups and downs; you can't predict the next moment in your life and what turn it will take.

I had excellent company with my friends, with whom I'd spent perfect quality time in early childhood.

You live your childhood in your old age again, and you would like to live it again and again, but your old friends might not be with you.

This time different old age hood friends from the other parts with a wide range of experiences to share with you with varying childhood stories, but everyone's objective would be the same: full entertainment, nothing else.

Many of my friends never visited school even once, they were illiterate, but it makes no difference to me because they were of good heart, and friendship was long-lasting with solid bonding.

One of my friends, Raju, was my first role model in life at that time.

Although he was entirely illiterate, even today, I greatly respect him because so many things were not possible to enjoy in those days without his courteous support due to military restrictions posted by my father.

He taught me many childhood life skills without going to school. It was a wonderfully rich experience that I learned from him.

A few of the skills were working in a team, sharing things, caring about the emotions of others (e.g., Emotional Quotients), celebrating festivals with limited resources, respect for elders, and so many for that you do not need any school education; it is an inherent family good culture that I learned from him in a very early age.

His father was our house owner, and we were renting his house. His mother was very kind and highly cultured, which may be why Raju had a sound value system.

I also greatly respected her because she was a social vigilance officer to guide me to become a good person.

You can't deliver your best if any person or your boss repeatedly interrupts your work.

It is true in your profession; you need some personal space for yourself, an inner circle in which you do not want anyone's interference if he is your father too.

You want to spend quality time on your own.

His restriction became a significant displeasure to me, and I started feeling that I did not have my own life.

I was under a dictatorship regime where you do not have the freedom to express yourself democratically.

One of my friends, Lachhman, had a similar dissatisfaction with his father, but with the different reasons of low-income family financial conditions; he wanted to do something extraordinary.

During this period, my other best friends, Mohan and Gopal, returned from an adventurous journey of fifteen days without informing their parents.

Their stories excited both of us. We were treating them like great personalities.

They returned from a major town trip, and we all didn't know about that; they had told their story full of enjoyment and pleasure with no restriction from their parents.

We had repeatedly asked them to share every minute detail during our daily evening meetings with all our friends.

I was also excited and thinking of doing extraordinary instantly to get rid of this controlled, restricted life.

Both were my motivational speaker and opinion leader. These are the top two personality traits of good leadership skills.

Can you imagine how human psychology works under stressful situations?

There is another management lesson; you must be calm if you are stressed.

When we had ensured that there would be no risk in going for an outbound trip that was going to be full of entertainment, one fine day, we both had to sit together to decide our next course of action.

Time was short and crucial to start acting immediately; we had decided to leave our houses the next day afternoon, planned so meticulously that Let there be no hindrance in the first journey to an outer unknown world.

That was a working day, my father, as usual, was in the office, and my mother, as per her routine practice, was in her afternoon long daydreaming napping.

Lachhman's father was out due to some work, and his elder sister was also; she used to work in a sugar mill. It was the first hurdle in our journey.

His sister used to leave for the company early in the morning and leave at 5 pm. Distance to this company was hardly two kilometers from our house.

We both left our respective houses by maintaining silence; many people who knew us very well were unaware that we would make a big blunder in our lives.

We had started moving slowly by making fun; at this age, we were unaware that there would be a need for food, cloth, and money. We were empty-handed with single wear cloth, nothing else.

We had never faced any adversity; hence we were not aware of the bitterness of life, even without having essential resources.

The first junction was my father's office; we had crossed that hurdle very safely.

I was aware that my father used to return from the office by 5 pm, so there was no challenge to us because earlier, many a time, I had traveled a kilometer distance to hand over a lunch box to my other friend's father's office, so it was not a challenge to me.

My friend's father's office was the next hurdle coming across us. After covering a distance of a kilometer, we reached our next destination.

We checked whether he was there from a long distance as he worked in the Municipal Corporation road toll check post; it is elementary to check anyone passing through this toll. There were two security present all the time.

Both of us were now very excited, but fear was troubling us as we had made the most significant decision of our life with no consultancy; we were the only person who knew about adventure.

We had very safely passed through that hurdle too. Life without any burden seems like skating over ice with no resistance to flow, and very easygoing when you can balance yourself against all odds while skating.

The success of the ladder is always full of challenges, and if you overcome all of them, you are the final winner, and there could be only one winner.

There is a saying that god helps only those who dare to take on tasks on and deliver as per plan and expected, planned results; the same thing was happening with both of us.

In this journey, our next station was my school. There was no problem with Lachhman because he never visited the school in his life; the real challenge was before me.

Although I was studying in middle school's morning session and at noon, there was a higher secondary session for higher classes.

There my elder brother Babloo was looking; we are three brothers. His classroom was facing the roadside.

I cautiously turned my face towards his class and tried to identify him from long distance view, but I could not catch him in a bunch of students inside the class.

I told him to run away immediately from this red zone area around 100 to 200 meters from his class, as I had earlier bitter experiences with my eldest brother.

Within a minute, we were luckily in the green zone again.

The road we had chosen was going to the state's top two most prominent cities.

However, those were almost fifty kilometers away from my town, and we could not realize it because I used to travel this distance once a year during summer vacation only when I used to go to my grandparent's home.

Now, we were about to reach another milestone, which was the factory of his elder sister, where she used to work as a daily wage worker in a sugar mill.

God and two other best friends, Good Luck and Bad Luck, watched every activity minutely, but suddenly, the scenario changed; there was a 180-degree turnaround.

I could not guess what started in my friend's mind—he slowed himself almost to rest and sit down there.

He might be tired and taking some rest to move ahead once again.

After a ten-minute's rest, I'd ask him again to get up, but he refused to do so, and to my surprise, it was unexpected to me to see his changed physical gestures.

The excited boy immediately became highly emotional. His emotional quotient was at the highest level; it was becoming challenging for me to pump excitement, motivation, and energy into him.

You can enhance your physical energy level by having an energy drink, but raising the bar of mental energy is challenging.

A person who has this level of emotion becomes the weakest. You can't deliver excellence with a high emotional quotient in the corporate world.

The same situation was to me. I was scared but controlled myself and asked the reason.

The reason that he told me brought tears to my eyes. You can't expect so much maturity from a boy who never visited the school, whatever he learned from the live life experience only.

He was crying. He controlled his emotion and told me he loved his elder sister too much.

Since he lost his mother a few years back, when he was three years old only, his elder sister was taking care of his whole family.

She was caring for their old ill father, younger brother, and one elder sister of mine. They had a minimal source of earning, and he will be the next person to add to the family income.

Somewhere, I felt that he realized his fault and understood the consequences of what he was trying to do.

He told me he couldn't continue with me and would instead go to meet his sister in the factory; if I wanted to continue, I could do it.

I was shocked and shattered my dream of living independently, but I was a different clay person. You can mold the clay and design your pot as per your requirement.

New management learning was that in your partnership business, people in life can be successful only when they are ready to face adversities and always prepared with plan B when plan A fails.

I'd left him there only and continued my journey alone; now, I had to make every decision independently and was entirely responsible for any miss-happening to me.

I'd started walking alone, but with some fear, I'd covered another mile. In those days, there was no mobile phone, so the modes of communication were limited. You could send messages through telegram and postcard only.

Now, you might be guessing what happened next.

I don't know whether he was a devil or god that came in front of me.

We never knew personally to each other, but later on, I recognized that he was a peon from my brother's school.

He bluntly asked with a bit of surprise, hey boy, where are you going alone on this road?

The question was imposed instantly, for that I had no answer; once again, I'd be scared.

I got broken into tears. The man scolded me to go back to home.

Tiny, helpless innocent Bunty turned around by 180 degrees again after seeing his angry face and ran away with a crying face, looking for Lachhman again.

Now, when I remember this incident again, I could realize that supreme power was standing in my way that was going to hell, and that power forced me to go back home and join the loving family again.

I am curious to know whether I was lucky or unlucky.

If I had moved further ahead, my luck could be a misfortune to me and might turn into a never-ending journey of lousy luck.

Finally, I turned back and returned to home.

Lachhman and I met many times later on; he was my neighbor. We never discussed this story with our friends in our daily briefing; there was a secret silence on our faces. We have hidden this secret in our hearts.

I'd never shared this incident throughout my life with anyone.

Only two of us were aware of that, but we had never discussed it with each other; it might be due to the lowest level of maturity we were carrying at that age.

Now first time sharing this story with you all after forty years of the incident.

Now how do you rate this story as full of thrill and suspense?

The Moral of a Story

"In your life, whenever you feel a lower level of motivation or under depression due to some adverse circumstances, start looking into the other side of the coin, which is happiness, believe in yourself, and try to become a master of circumstances."

Chapter 5

Severe Illness > First Interaction with God

"Sometimes you will be in control of your illness, and other times you'll sink into despair, and that's ok! Freak out, forgive yourself, and try again tomorrow".

Kelly Hemingway, an Ice Skater.

Courtesy: Image source Severe Illness: Dreamstime

In this world, no one wants to be ill. Peoples are highly health cautious and use all tools and techniques to stay fit because treatment costs are enormously high compared to the cost of staying healthy.

Nowadays, the world is full of health-related information and advanced treatment facilities.

Medical treatment facilities are readily available with little expense due to various health insurance schemes, the government's health insurance policies for poor people, and medical expenses affordability.

It was not the case three to four decades earlier; you had to rely on limited medical facilities and doctor resources.

Treatment facilities were available at Government hospitals only.

Fatality rates were high due to poor hygiene conditions. People also needed to be more aware of maintaining good hygiene conditions.

Earlier, there was no such family planning concept; hence, more prominent extended families resulted in shared limited resources.

There was no dedicated special attention to each child due to the more prominent family; hence the possibility of getting ill was very high.

A poor innocent boy like me, who was starting to understand this world, and the seeding of ambition was about to commence.

As I shared my adventures, you found success and failure.

It was a different experience, once again, full of good and bad luck.

These two words are the title theme of this book, and they will repeatedly appear at regular intervals.

When I was 10, during my summer holidays, I was at my maternal grandfather's home and enjoying lovely days with my cousin and friends.

I was not a very healthy boy with a good physique. I was a fragile and poor-health boy who loved to believe in living with doctors very often.

Surrounding poor hygiene conditions was the predominant factor responsible for these routine trips to next to God, i.e., the Doctor.

You may call like that God loved to see me time and again through the Doctor's eye.

It was another way of caring and meeting with me.

That was a different kind of so much closeness & love affair with them.

There is a saying that too much is terrible everywhere in every stage of life.

Discipline is the need for a healthy life.

This time I was not aware that different was written in my destiny, and I will not be a lucky young chap who used to come out victorious from the routine use of medicines time and again.

I got ill once again, as usual, traveling to the Doctor began.

My family and I were very confident that this was a matter for a few days and I would get back to my routine as Medicine was my perfect and close friend; it was proximity between the two of us, but on an evil day your lovely friend may turn the face and may stand in the opposite side of you.

My all-weather best friend, Medicine, was this time standing along with bad luck, who always tried to put me down at every opportunity.

My good friend Medicine started behaving like a bad friend, who was very angry this time due to some unknown reason I don't know.

Even after a week time, there was no friendship between the two of us. I'd repeatedly requested to continue our good long-lasting relationship but to no avail.

When a good friendship turns worse, it directly impacts your health for psychological reasons. Now the same had started happening to me.

My family was surprised this time as it was deteriorating daily rather than getting a health improvement.

Medicine was not responding correctly, and a consistently high fever of hundred plus was raising concern among all family members.

My other lovely friends were sad, and they stopped playing and started praying for my early recovery.

The Doctor was helpless; family members were fearsome. If I could remember, it was a typhoid; if not treated on time, it could be a fatal disease.

The Doctor was losing hope. They tried their best, but my immune system, day by day, was getting weaker and weaker.

It was almost a month passed, and now my relatives started losing hope for my survival and started thinking about the end of this life cycle due to the very rare probability of recovery.

My mother silently prayed with hidden tears in her eyes, but she was very confident. I'd miraculously saved in many earlier incidents.

My mother believed that it would also not happen this time if it didn't happen earlier.

Some years back, one child of the same age lost the battle of their life.

Now I could have been another victim in no time. Will this happen this time in our family?

It was apparent that poor sanitation was responsible for my current situation, so you can't blame anyone.

Nowadays, we are cautious about health hygiene ourselves as well as our kids; in those days, this was not the situation.

The countdown started, and it was almost a month passed, and I was in bed.

Now prayer started superseding Medicine. In the Indian Hindu culture, there is a belief that when Medicine does not work, then start praying to God to work for you.

We can't imagine the power of spirituality or the ability of attraction; whether you believe it or not, if you pray to God honestly, the whole universe starts working for you by heart.

You might be laughing, but this is true; many videos are now available on

YouTube to witness the power of attraction.

A pure soul of a small child is the representation of God.

If a minor child smiles, think God is smiling and pouring love over you.

A ten-year-old child is an innocent soul; God always loves their creation.

In Indian mythology, there is a belief in reincarnation, and wrong or good things happening in people's current life depend upon the good and bad things done in their past lives.

There is a bank balance of a good blessing account in every-one's life, and as and when badly needed, it is used.

Another saying is that no one can harm you if God is with you.

One of my maternal grandmothers had a high level of faith in one of the very aged saints residing near our house.

She used to visit there every Thursday to attend special praying there. I'd also gone once there and took his spiritual blessing the year before.

I was on my last bed this time and counting my remaining breathing.

She immediately visited there and took the spiritual blessing from him and gave it to me.

Medical science might be surprised and might declare this ridiculous.

Medical science also understands that happiness and sadness generate in our body due to the formation of some chemicals; if this can happen, why can't good faith generate similar chemicals and cure the diseases done by Medicine?

I am not a doctor, but I have understood that if you visit any doctor, his smile, caring behavior, and confidence cure half of the disease.

A miracle happened. You might believe it or not, but it happened.

As I shared the title of this chapter as my first interaction with God that evening, surprisingly, I started dreaming of direct interaction with all holy gods and goddesses; they were smiling at me and sharing their happiness with me.

It was a rare moment that happened to anyone.

It seems funny or joking, but it is authentic and genuine.

An Unknown supernatural power connects the world, which we can feel but can't see.

In the next three to four hours, I started recovering with the same medicines not working earlier.

I'd started murmuring the name of God; more than twenty people surrounded me I could not have remembered.

Every one surprised that I was sharing my experience of God with them.

Life is lovely; you have to learn the technique of living.

After passing so many years, my good karmic account had a better blessing balance than an imperfect blessing that positively impacted my life.

Finally, I came out from this immense life-threatening experience of my whole life; it never reoccurred later on in my entire life. Touch wood.

This time again, both good and bad luck were crying but had tears of happiness, as bad luck always tried to put me down but never wanted me to fail permanently.

It was a swing situation, not a one-sided game.

Still, do you think God is nowhere? No, my friend, it is everywhere and always ready to help you out when you are in trouble; the only condition is you have to work the same way for others.

He loves his every creation and takes care of them all the time.

Your excellent work always returns you, like your investment too early or later, but yes.

After that, I got sick again many times later, but that was a minor illness, and I came out as a winner every time.

Did you like this incredible, funny journey of my life?

The Moral of a Story

"Life is beautiful; take the maximum benefits of this, help people, do good things, and care for your health. If your health is good, you can do wonder. Good or bad things you have done are long-lasting; it will return you with compounding interest; now you have to decide which part you want to keep with you, good or bad; the decision is yours".

Chapter 6

Summer Holiday Vs. Summer Exam > What to Choose

"What do I want to take home from my summer vacation? Time. The wonderful luxury of being at rest. The days when you shut down the mental machinery that keeps life on track and lets life wander. The days when you stop planning, analyzing, thinking, and just are. Summer is my period of grace".

Ellen Goodman, an American journalist, and syndicated columnist

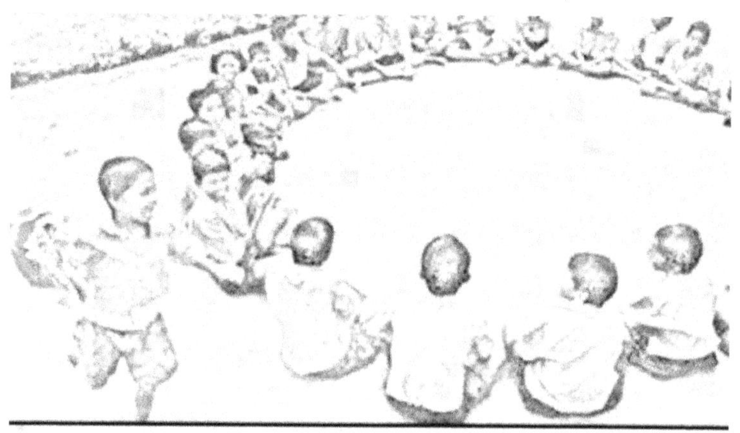

Courtesy: Image source Summer Holidays: Odia live

For every school-going child, summer vacation is a mouth-watering festival.

After the hectic full calendar academic schedule, you finally face the challenging exam for approximately a month, and then you get mentally fully exhausted; then, after this mental stress, you need a break to rejoice again.

You have to go through a waiting period to get the examination result.

With all the sensation, thrill, drama, and curiosity, you reach school to get the final report card that decides your mode of enjoyment for the forthcoming summer vacation.

This yearly cycle continues until your academic career's final exam ends, and you move forward to the next life cycle.

It is a long, tedious journey; with every step you take, this pattern changes with your age and surrounding circumstances.

I was not an exceptional boy but also going through the same cycle.

That year, I appeared in the 8th state board examination. It was a very prestigious exam because the results of this decide your career path, whether you want to be a Doctor, Engineer, Charter accountant, or wish to enter into some other stream like Law, etc.

In those days, Doctors and engineers were highly respected people in society. The feeling is still the same.

I also dreamed of being an Engineer because I loved mathematics too much.

It was my favorite subject and the first step to becoming an Engineer; in those days, it was a dream for most of the child.

As soon as I had completed my examination in the first week of April, I started packing luggage with my mother & siblings to go for a most awaited entire amusement-only journey of the year to my maternal grandparent's home.

Everyone was highly excited, and so was I.

Every year we used to stay on summer vacation for a minimum of two months there with full uninterrupted enjoyment right from child games, playing cards, watching movies, animal circus, and attending social gatherings because that period was of the marriage season, attending various festivals, and visiting in the city.

Our activity used to go on from 8 AM till 10 PM. Our maternal grandparents often scolded us for disturbing their noon sleep. Still, finally, they loved us a lot because we also brought happiness into their life for a short period only.

We were a group of approximately twenty children, and our activities varied daily to maintain interest throughout the summer.

Traveling by bus after a day of preparation, we all in the afternoon reached our amusement center with a high level of excitement and energy; after all, we were meeting with our friends after a gap of one year, and in those days, there was no source of communication like WhatsApp to do a video chat and get all updates.

It was our only face-to-face meeting after a long gap.

Our news of reaching there spread @ light speed in every corner of the locality.

It was a time of full enjoyment; everyone was free from yearlong complex studies.

Everyone knew we had minimal time and had to use this adventure time fully.

We reached there fifteen days before the declaration of the results. It was the only hurdle for all of us because this would decide your level of amusement in the next two months.

Anyway, that time they arrived when everyone had forgotten their enjoyment for some time and went out to get their respective report card.

I was confident of passing with distinction and getting the best ranking in the school.

Our school declared the result on 30th Apr. As usual, my father represented me in the school, and as he expected, I got the top rank in the 8th Board exam. I was once again a school topper. Once again, my father, with a blown chest and heart, reached home with a report card and sent us a communication through our lonely bus ticket checker, sharing the report card and my top rank.

I was the only boy in the group with this prestigious recognition. Could you imagine the level of happiness? I could not contain this enormous energy level within me; it came out with an uncontrolled flood and covered all surroundings.

Although all my friend got cleared their respective level examination by getting different grades, we shared our report cards and spent the whole day discussing this only.

The next day, we were again celebrating and forgot yesterday.

In management, there is a saying: forget your past and take care of your present to build your future.

We all started taking care of our present and dived ourselves into the deep ocean of happiness.

Nature was pleased and was pouring her love into all.

As I said, to build the future, you had to take care of your present; the same thing would happen to me.

I was not aware that destiny had a different idea that was not part of my plan because I was not that kid who got matured before the age.

I always believed in enjoying life to the full extent.

The very next day, I got a message from my father; on that day, the mode of communication was only through postal cards.

I couldn't understand whether he was my godfather or something else who always came before me and my freelance life.

The message was unambiguous. I was shocked. I'd never imagined that this would happen to me; my dreams got shattered, and I got lost utterly for a moment.

There was a complete dark around me for a moment, and no one was immediately there who could condone me.

I couldn't think how to react; shall I cry or accept the reality of life? I had to choose between the two.

Happiness and sadness can't be on a single side of a coin. One is on the brighter side, and the other is on the darker side.

This message was communicated to me by my maternal uncle, who always used to make a joke with me, especially when I received a report card.

Initially, I thought this was another joke played by him with me.

He always told me that I had a good rank in the school because my father is in the police department, and he influenced teachers every year for the same, but that was not the truth.

But I knew my father's sincerity; he rarely made the joke with anyone. He was earnest in his communication.

He was very determined and caring to all of us, so the matter was grave.

You might be thinking about what exactly the matter was that became so serious.

In a clear message, my father ordered me to return home in the middle of the holiday the next day.

There was only one bus that went to my village. I had to leave the next day by 2 PM. I had left with only 24 hours to joy, which turned into a sad scenario.

The reason for my return was to appear in the state-level talent search competitive exam conducted only once after the 8th board examination in a lifetime.

Once you are through, you can get admission to the best schools in the state.

Apart from selection, there was a long scholarship till the completion of my graduation. The scholarship amount was higher than my father's monthly salary.

It could be a triumphant moment for him if I got selected; this was a lifetime opportunity for me.

I had to compete for the few positions in the whole state; if I missed this chance, my dream to become Engineer could be vanished or weakened.

Those days there was no telephone or mobile to discuss directly with my teacher and get their advice or discuss with a career counselor.

Nowadays, parent sends their ward to suitable coaching classes with good career planning.

Since I was from a tiny town, I was only aware that if I took mathematics as the main subject, I will be on the path to Engineering College through another competitive exam.

I was in a dilemma, whether it was good luck or bad luck for me. Option one returned, and appearing in the examination was good luck, or staying here only may be bad luck to me.

A million-dollar question at that age, and I had to answer with a whole level of maturity; there was no one with whom I should seek advice as I was a timid guy.

Finally, late at night, I decided.

That was the most challenging decision of my life at this age: to return for my given long-term best career opportunity that was my dream and leave aside my short-term amusement.

I also learned another management lesson which I realized now that if you want to get the highest level in your career, you have to learn to sacrifice small leisure for the moment.

Once you reach your destiny, that leisure will come before you again, which you missed during that struggling period.

Life is wonderful. What do you think? Every moment you will find it is full of thriller and suspense.

I don't know who was smiling, my good luck or bad luck, but based on experience, both were very happy this time.

Bad luck was happy because I couldn't enjoy it, and my friend's good fortune was also pleased because I had made the right decision to return.

Finally, I'd appear in the examination; we got the result after fifteen days.

This time I was with my father. It was the first time I was getting first-hand results along with him rather than getting through my funny maternal uncle.

The day when I got my result, another moment, I could not react once again; I could not believe it. I'd never thought that this was also possible.

Who was there, who was so much caring about me?

I got the first rank in the state in the state talent search examination.

I was a state topper; I could not believe in myself and my capability, but my father knew right from my early schooling days as he used to get feedback from my teachers.

It was the first time I could feel my father's feelings and happiness and the first time I found him smiling.

My parent poured all their love into me.

There was another triumphant moment for the family; there were tears of happiness in everyone's eyes, including our landlord; although she was illiterate, she always cared for me whenever she found me going out of track.

She was my first life teacher. She is no longer now; in the later stage of life,

I'd again met her. She has been my inspiration throughout my life, and I will have great respect for her till my last breath.

Finally, I got admission to the best school in the state, and my next trip was full of broken hearts and excitement. I left my beautiful town and my dear friends forever, and after that, there was no return back.

Now if I remember those days, I found that most of my friends left this world at an early age for a new journey of life without even once meeting with me, and I'll always regret it.

The Moral of a Story

"Your ultimate superpower already defines your destiny. You must move accordingly against all your wishes. Do your karma, and results will follow you".

Chapter 7

Board Exam> My Favorite Missing

"Success is not final; failure is not fatal: it is the courage to continue that counts."

Winston Churchill, former Prime Minister of the United Kingdom

Courtesy: Image Source Board Exam: Newsnation. in

Board exams: shivering, shivering, and only shivering.

It is such a kind of fear, anxiety, and terror that you feel sweat even in winter, and what would be the climax of all there when you are about to enter an examination hall?

All of you have gone through this phase time and again.

This exam happens to be your future path decider; with one mistake, you might miss the bus, and you have to go through another same psychological process for preparation and reappear next year for the same kind of mental test process.

What I understand from many peoples, talked to them that there is every chance that your memory disappears just after receiving the examination paper.

The winner is the one who maintains calm and relaxed and starts cautiously writing answers.

Many peoples shared with me that they are still scared of the exams in their dream even after decades passed. Still, they feel that they appear in the same exam repeatedly, and every time disqualified from reaching the examination center or get different subject papers not prepared for that.

You may be one of them or lucky you do not have this exam phobia.

Only psychologists can tell the reason and address this issue.

I am writing all this. There would be a reason behind this; you might think that I should have mentioned my favorite book title this time. Bad luck – good luck.

Could you imagine this book reaching its final destination without this lovely adventure?

This book might have less number of pages, but the stories are so funny that everyone at some other time will feel part of this.

In my school days, I have gone through this phase three times. Per my state's education system, I had to appear for the board examination in classes 5th, 8th, and 11th.

In my first adventure, as communicated earlier, I was the school topper throughout my schooling session.

There was a great expectation from me in the 5th board examination.

I was always scared of geography; it was not my favorite subject.

I had prepared for each and every chapter very meticulously, except for a couple of things I'll share with you later on; this is just to maintain curiosity and excitement.

There were four papers, the first three were in Mathematics, Science, and Language, and I did well. Now my confidence was on a seventh sky.

In sporting language, if you are doing very well consistently, then it is said that you are in the best of your form.

For example, international tennis players ranked no.1 grabbed the grand slam in one calendar year and maintained a sustainable world no. 1 ranking for a long time.

It was the last paper, and I was confident finishing it with a bang.

I reached the examination hall with a complete smile and confidence.

As soon as the exam paper reached my hand and I went through it, I was shocked to see that one of the questions was purely on the map, and I had to mark the few crucial monuments on the country map.

I did not prepare for this else; I had prepared for each category. Legs had started cold sweating. The topper position was slipping from my hand.

It was a do-or-die situation.

Bad luck again came in and started smiling; poor good luck was hiding the face and was sitting in a corner but, like a winner, never quits, started thinking about me to help me out.

There is a saying that if god is with you, nothing can harm you.

This time, I just remembered my teacher's vital tip of my teacher first cool down once you have gone through the question paper and mark those questions that you can attempt very quickly, and then concentrate on those tough questions that require some mental toughness.

I forgot the fear and finished the easy one very fast, and now I had sufficient time for this only tough one that required extraordinary skill.

I practice excellently correlating every point with some picture or story during study time.

I started recovering monuments with some related stories and locations.

I recalled each one and placed it on a country map successfully.

Finally, I was a winner and retained my No.1 title.

How was this one? This time winner was again good luck; this was a clear case of a drowning person who got life support from a tiny help.

The second story was about my 8th board examination; now, this time, the turn was on mathematics, one of my favorite subjects, and was crucial for reaching my Engineering destination.

I sometimes needed help remembering the math theorem. I believe in understanding the concept rather than recognizing it by repeated reading.

There were ten theorems in the syllabus, and I had no choice but to remember all as per my studying practice of getting 100 % ready for all the subjects.

Dear friend, this time I missed the bus, just before the examination I could remember only nine theorems and the last one remained.

What to do?

What will happen if this is part of the question paper the next day?

Honest and hardworking people never cheat on themselves. They always respect the voice of their soul.

This time, I confess that I had tried to cheat my soul for the first time.

I don't know whether this was the innovative way, but I'd created a unique way of cheating because I did not want to fail.

There was a great stack in my reputation, and I tried to maintain my reputation as a topper.

No one had tried this trick globally; this was a unique invention with the help of using the principle of science I had just started learning without any practical experimentation, as in those days in school, there was no science lab.

There is a saying; necessity is the mother of invention.

I found that carrying paper notes in my trouser pocket would direct trouble if the invigilator examined them.

So I decided to do it differently. In mathematics, you always need a pencil box with other supporting tools.

I used the inside bottom of the box for my cheating and innocently wrote the last theorem with an ink pen; it was not easily visible.

Those days there were only physical checking of student for carrying any objectionable supporting paper to write an exam.

This time, I was worried in the examination hall based on my last board exam experience.

When the question paper came into my hand, what happened?

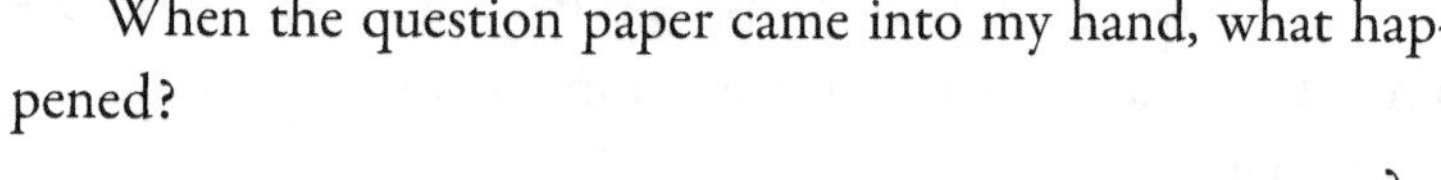

This devil theorem was there, smiling over me and asking me where will you go now, my topper? Theorem had caught the champion now

Oh! My goodness or badness.

But this was my time to smile now. Good and bad luck, both were surprised that I was smiling in this challenging situation. Both my friends couldn't guess what will be my next move.

I'd checked the outside world cautiously, opened my pencil box, and looked toward my unique creative work. Work finished, the winner never loses again, and the loser never wins.

Was it so easy for me to finish the task so sophistically?

No, never, guys Ink that I'd used to write the theorem was completely dried.

It was tough to see the geometry drawing and text. In those days, shiny ink ball pen was not very popular, or you could say it were not available in the small town.

The world is growing exponentially just because a few intellectuals challenged existing practices and wrote a new story on the wall of success.

The world has saluted them for their contribution; the Nobel award is one kind of appreciation for their unique work that forever helped humanity.

Since I was a science student, I'd read about the optics of light, especially the reflection of light.

I'd used the same science theory and tilted my pencil box so that sunlight entering from the window incident over ink, and by the reflection of light, I could see the geometry and text. Luckily I was sitting on a widow's side.

Now imagine how science can be helpful in a different way. It would be best if you were a master of circumstance.

Am I fortunate? Yes. In every phase of life, the practical application of learned knowledge is more valuable instead just remembering the theory and never experimenting with it.

My younger son nowadays holds the baton of implementing theoretical learning in solving our day-to-day technical problems.

My third experience with the board exam was in the 11th board exam.

This time it was English. English is not my mother tongue; it was just a subject for me, and I had to clear with a big score. Now as a Professional, it is my bread and butter.

In this competitive world, additional language fluency is mandatory for

success, especially in reading, writing, and speaking English.

I was appearing in a board exam in my mother tongue language medium.

You can understand the difficulty if you don't have mastery of the subject, or you can say if you do not have reading, writing, and speaking skills.

I prepared myself with the same pressure to become the topper again.

This time essay writing was the challenge, I had prepared many essays for the exam, or I just repeatedly remembered the article's flow without understanding the meaning of each sentence.

I was in the examination hall again, and now the English paper was in my hand; as usual, I had gone through the question paper and found everything was in place except all remembered essays.

All those essays were missing.

You know the contribution of the essay in the paper is almost twenty percent.

You can imagine my situation once again. Because of this silly question, my overall marks average went down by at least four percent, a considerable number in a significant competitive examination.

How to handle such a situation when nothing is in your hand? Hopeless situation.

Whom should I blame, a teacher who did not teaches us well or our education system that does not prepare the student to overcome psychologically from this situation?

In such a situation, only your mental stability and presence of mind could save you.

It could be the most challenging last board-level examination of anyone's life.

This time I'd sat silently and kept this question on hold as a last question to solve. I quickly finished all the other questions and kept half an hour free for this last question.

In the paper, I had to write an essay on any of three subjects; one subject was on any sport, rest two I just remembered.

Fortunately, a few months back, I heard the running commentary of the final hockey match between my country and another country.

It was a seventy-minute match in both English and my mother tongue.

I'd recalled all the incidents of that match and, without fear of excellent or wrong grammar, wrote down the whole essay in the last thirty minutes uninterrupted.

Nowadays, in spoken English, how many of us take care of correct grammatical English while speaking?

You should communicate your thoughts to the audience effectively. It is the only requirement.

Good luck again in winning the match; I got excellent marks in English with retaining the number one rank.

Are these not commendable tasks?

How much would you rate this another real story?

You would be laughing that now I wrote this book in English.

You might be questioning flow and grammatical mistakes, but still, I can share my thoughts in the best possible way to learn and understand language.

It is a real blessing from all of you.

The Moral of a Story

"In the phase of your life, you have to appear for many exams, sometimes you are well prepared to overcome hurdles that come across you, and sometimes challenges are before you, and for that, you are not fully prepared. Your only past knowledge or experience is the key to success in handling such tricky situations".

Chapter 8

Engineering Selection > Gamble or Confidence

"Many of life's failures are people who did not realize how close they were to success when they gave up."

Thomas Edison, a Scientist

Courtesy: Image source Engineering selection: QS (Top University)

Gambling if I say it is a good thing to do, no one will agree as the probability of failure is very high, and the chances of success are meager.

It is a game of luck; sometimes, you are a winner or a loser.

Everyone can't be a great gambler whose success rate is very high. You can't play this game all the time without following unethical practices. You have to be tricky and have very good data analytical skills along with good luck.

On a fine day, you are a winner, but on another bad day, you are a loser.

Life is also a game of gambling, and you have to play even if you do not wish or you have to force to do.

We have to do this for the betterment of our life.

This was another adventure of my life; I don't know whether, once again, it would be a good or bad outcome.

This time, I was a fifteen years' adolescent, neither a boy nor an adult; that was the transition phase of the age.

Changing the path once opted in is difficult when looking for better career opportunities.

My dream was to become a successful Engineer in my professional life.

I appeared in another 11th board examination. In less than a month, I had to appear for the Pre-engineering entrance test examination.

There were hardly 1000 seats in the whole state, and there were more than three hundred thousand students who were taking this test. The probability of success was only 0.33 percent.

It was one of the most prestigious exams; clearing this was every student's dream.

I always found myself as a daydreamer; you may call it the law of attraction that whatever you want to achieve in your life, you have to start realizing and behaving like that even way before you reach the same.

This is the concept of nature's kindness to every human being I'd learned in middle age, but its beauty is that I'd started practicing way back at an early age without knowing its alphabet.

I'd started dreaming of being an Engineer and behaving like that only. I was highly confident to be successful. I had declared myself a successful candidate for the engineering course before cracking the examination.

In the meantime, one more success story was waiting for me and my family.

After the PET (Pre Engineering Test) exam, I received the board exam result.

Once again, I had the top with first rank in the whole district in the science stream.

My friend good luck was in a celebration mood, and suddenly he started singing, "Congratulations, let's celebration, Congratulations, let's celebration."

Can anyone have so much good luck? But behind the scene, there was great hard work and compromises with all leisure; there were only hard work, hard work, and only hard work.

My eldest brother was my opinion leader.

Nowadays, there is a great value of an opinion leader. People desperately follow their thought.

He was the person who ignited the flame to become an engineer within me.

My elder brother Babloo, who was my inspiration throughout my academic career, he all the time stood behind me to help me out of all difficulties.

There was always a surprise that he rarely appreciated me; I was sure he was not jealous of me because I brought happiness to the family many times.

Just before the declaration of results, admission to the Science Graduation College would start.

My brother came to me and asked what my plan was.

I am surprised about what he is asking. It was already apparent to everyone, even my close family circle.

He was very serious, came close to me, and whispered in my ears, this is the golden opportunity for you to take the admission as the due date is about to expire before the declaration of my engineering entrance test result.

If I missed this opportunity, I have to wait for a year to get admission because admission to other reputed science colleges was closed, and this was the last opportunity for me.

I do not know whether it was a joke or he was not very much confident about me because he was not successful in the earlier attempts of this exam.

He was playing safe with me and showing protective or possessive behavior with me. He was always very highly protective of me.

Once again, I was in a dilemma. On the one hand, there was a safe opportunity; on the other hand, your dream awaited you.

There were only two days left, and after five days, the result was about to declare.

His repetitive follow-up was shaking my confidence, or in other words, it was also the testing time for my mental toughness. That time I was passing through the litmus test.

Nowadays corporate working culture, success follows only those who are mentally strong during their tough time.

This management lesson took my litmus test, and I had to go through this.

Those were sleepless days and nights for me; I could hardly sleep for three to four hours in a day, and this lasted for more than two months.

If I succeeded, I would be the first engineer in my family. Otherwise, I would become a person living an everyday life in a crowd of millions.

Finally, I made up my mind, decided and go to sleep, took a complete rest after the hectic schedule of so many days, and with a fresh sense, I announced my decision that I would not opt the option of a Science graduation course, instead, I will wait for the entrance test result.

This was my strategy, and still, I am following to take a tough call late in the night and go for a sound sleep, and announce decisions early in the morning.

Days, Hours, minutes, and seconds passed, and finally, the moment came; in those days, there was no internet or computer or laptop, and results used to be printed in the newspaper only.

My brother brought the newspaper, and without reading that, he declared that there was no good news for me.

But I was very calm and silent and was keenly observing his every moment focused my eyes on his face, and I was trying to read his face that was not linked with his speech.

Although I am not a psychiatrist but able to read his second face, somewhere I'd observed that he was lying to me.

After a few seconds, he said it was better to check for the polytechnic, as there was a possibility for me based on the year-long hard work done by me, as this would be a consolation to me.

He took away my admission card number and started tracking it in the newspaper.

He had spent almost ten to fifteen minutes and put his head down with the highest level of depression and hopeless gestures; with a sad face, he declared that I am failed in my effort and started taunting me that I did not follow his advice for earlier admission, now what you will do.

I was still calm and silent; no harsh weather can put you down when you are confident enough.

I believed in the world-famous saying fake it till you make it.

It is the law of attraction; it is a proven tool no one can have denied it.

As per this law, I had already seen myself as an Engineer, and no one could fail me; it was my firm belief because I had already made an effort to make this happen.

My mother asked and ordered him to see the next engineering section.

He was hesitant and unconfident about me but started to recheck my roll number with an almost dismal face.

I concentrated my eyes on his face; in my life, I was so cautious the first time, but in one corner of my heart word "No'" started roaming; after a few minutes, everything was in black and white.

In a fraction of a second, I observed a very tiny cute smile on his face, but immediately he hides the same and declares without facing anyone with head down that he was sorry you couldn't.

Everyone momentarily lost consciousness, but I smiled like a different man.

Now it was my time.

I told my brother that my roll number is M5050, and I needed to verify the same; he acted to handover the newsletter to me, and as soon as I'd reached it, he pulled away from reach of mine and threw it in the air, jumped with all joy, lifted me, and finally announced that I got selected for the Engineering course.

There was another moment of tears of happiness in everyone's eyes, it was not mine, but my parent's dream came true.

I'd cried as a small kid, but it was a moment of celebration. After all, I was the first person in my family who got this success.

My gamble worked very well; I was on the seventh sky.

Gamble and confidence worked together for me. It was a win-win situation.

In this journey, my disciplined visionary father was the winner; his long-lasting efforts finally yielded a fruitful result.

Today he is no more with us, already left years back for the heavenly journey; I am dedicating this story to my beloved father.

The Moral of a Story

"If there is the will to do something, there are always many ways, and if you are confident in the success of your ambitious life target, be stuck with that; no one can deviate you from your path."

Chapter 9

First Job at Twenty> Tips for Survival

Don't be afraid to give your best to what seemingly are small jobs. Every time you conquer one, it makes you that much stronger. If you do the little jobs well, the big ones will tend to take care of themselves.

William Patten, an author and scholar.

Courtesy: Image source First job: Extra Mile

Our journey of life begins with our first life event.

This first would be of any kind, whether it is our first walk on our foot or our first day of school, our first friend, our first teacher, our first college picnic trip, our first love, our first day after marriage, our first child, our first car, our first house, and there are countless first in our life.

If we start thinking, we will drown in the sweet memories of many first.

Every first has its own experience and long-lasting memory.

Enjoyment of your first can not be explained or expressed in words; it is boundary-less, beyond the imagination.

Last but not least, one of your life's most essential memorable incidents is once you graduate or post-graduate and get your first job opportunity.

The feeling of getting the first job opportunity is just like being in heaven, and god fulfills all our wishes.

In this society, there is no respect for the person doing nothing; it seems like a burden on society as they are not adding value to the community or nation.

Once you are employed, you become a member of a society that treats you respectfully else thinks like garbage.

Until you are a student, no one is bothered about you as there is no financial expectation. Still, as soon as you become eligible for earning, the way of thinking of society takes a U-turn and automatically raises the bar of expectation.

Delayed in getting any source of earning, you immediately become the talk of the town in society for your unemployment, and this is one of the worst situations for any educated, employed youth.

Since I was doing one of the most prestigious Engineering degree courses, the expectations of getting a very luxurious job with a handsome salary even before graduation started to build pressure on me as soon as I finished the course.

Everyone had started thinking that I was from a premium class, so employers shall immediately pour the entire basket of job opportunities, and I would pick up one of the best as per will.

If life were so simple, then there would be no hindrance in the world; everyone would live a peaceful life with no clashes, and everyone was happy with each other.

But this world is full of challenges, which are present everywhere.

So how could I isolate myself from this?

During Engineering, I had a big dream to become a successful Engineer.

I graduated with a good score, ranked in the college, and became eligible for the campus interview.

One of the company's HR visited our college, I had produced my candidature before them, and I was very confident to grab this opportunity.

Once you are out of college, you think that the world is waiting for you to take open-handed, but the reality is ruthless; your honeymoon period is over, and now you have to learn to portray yourself as an essential asset to your employer, and you are the best available option among all.

I, along with my other friends, appeared for the interview; some of them had excellent academic records and presentation skills.

Everyone did very well and tried to impress a recruiter with their technical and other soft skill, but it could have worked better.

To everyone's surprise, even it was a surprise to our teachers too, that everyone rejected.

It was the first but most significant setback for all of us; the first potential recruiter had challenged our five-year degree knowledge in on-campus interviews. No one could believe this.

Our college placement cell officer had told us that this would be our first and last campus interview; no other organization was showing interest in us. In those days' firms hardly believed in campus recruitment, unlike nowadays.

It was a direct message to all of us that now we were thrown into the deep sea and we had to learn the art of survival on our own without any life support; it was like a baby fish with her first breath starts swimming on her own in the water, there is no formal training, no trainer or coach there.

The same was beginning to happen to me; people living around my home started asking me when I would get my first job.

If you are a skilled, experienced person and in demand – the supply game, if the balance is tilting towards need, in simple words, if the demand is more than supply, you are the most welcome person; everyone would love to keep you in their ship at your terms, but it was not the case with me.

There is a saying that success has many fathers but failure is an orphan;

However, I was not a failure person; there was nothing else with me except my graduation degree, no experience, no skill, how and why anyone would notice you.

Finally, no one noticed me; in those days, there were no internet or job sites where you could register yourself for seeking, at a glance, job opportunities.

The level of professionalism could have been higher; no one was bothered about you or what you had done.

It was a clear message to me that I had to start this journey.

There was only one option left for me to get the reference and the job. It was also not so easy in those days. Personal contacts were not readily available due to poor resources of communication.

I'd spoken to my eldest brother; we are three brothers.

He got some of his friend's friend references, who had initiated a startup in the early nineties, and asked me to contact him, but the problem was that he was in the other town more than 300 kilometers away from my house.

I had to visit alone, and I'd never done this before. I had no idea how to reach there and meet the guy of reference; we had never been introduced to each other early.

I had minimal information and had to explore to get there.

Early in the morning, my brother gave me a send-off at the railway station with a small token amount of money, hardly equivalent to one dollar; now, if I provide the same amount to my kids, they directly refuse even to touch them.

You can now understand my situation.

I was on a blind journey; it was just like in the middle of the sea with no bank around; no one knew where shall am I leading.

A scared 20 years old gentleman was about to write his destiny on his own with no godfather to help him out from any trouble.

Now I had to make decisions independently; I was lonely and responsible for any good or bad outcomes.

If I returned from the mid of the journey, the future was blinking and dark; I had to find the source of a tiny light of the hope that I would do it.

It was another biggest challenge in my life.

I have a deep belief in god; one of my father's friends regularly visited our house, and they used to have long discussions, and during the debate, he always used one sentence repeatedly, which I earned many times from him.

His famous sentence was, "If you're a daring person, there is the value of your daring, not that man's value. People always value your daring only."

This daring comes from your confidence that nothing is impossible on this earth.

This single sentence, which I heard many times in my early childhood life, helped boost my confidence.

I decided to face this world and repeatedly told myself that I would survive, stay, and survive.

I reached my first destination by train, brought my luggage, and got to the bus station; there was another challenge before me: I was going to the other state where the spoken language was different from what I had never heard before.

It was just like compounding trouble for me. I faced a challenge identifying which bus would go to my final destination because the signboards were in the local, regional language.

Anyhow I caught the bus and reached there, but the challenges tested me repeatedly.

Bus had no direct stop at my final destination; they dropped me on the highway and asked to take help from local people.

I could explain my address and get directions in English and my mother tongue.

After half an hour of struggle, those days there was no Google map to track your destination precisely, I reached there.

On arrival, I got an excellent welcome and good food on the first day; I was introduced to labor working in that gentleman's company, helping me get my first job.

He was a good-hearted person and well-behaved.

After three days of yes or no, its and buts, I got the first job opportunity that was hardly equivalent to twenty dollars a month.

To keep fit, you need food at least twice daily.

For the first week, I stayed there only in the company office. It was a full-fledged office in the day, but at night, it was my bedroom.

You can't sleep without food because I had to work hard daily for twelve hours, six days a week.

The demand for good food was very high, but I needed more money to get this.

In those days' laborers were also staying in that gentleman's company campus, and they were from my state only; they could speak my language and understand me and my difficulties, and for a whole week, those good-hearted people offered me dinner without any return expectation.

I'd stayed there for a week, and I was a deplorable guy who had nothing to give them in return for their priceless good service except my best wishes & blessing to them as they were representatives of god for me.

I tasted a wide variety of good quality food later in my life, but it is, to date, tough to forget the long-lasting taste of those foods made with love because it was the question of survival for life, and there were no other options.

The company for which I was working offered me shelter in the company premises itself as I could not financially afford to take a house on rent outside, but this was at the cost of the comfort of my coworker; they vacated their restroom happily for me only.

Later on, we had buildup very good binding and relationships.

I made many friends in those days; all were genuine and good-hearted.

Now, I had no dinner treat; I had to arrange my own; most of the time, dinner ended on either snack or fruit only with a partially filled stomach.

I learned many survival lessons; I continued my job for around five months.

That period made me a mature professional, and I acquired many technical and soft skills, which are now mandatory requirements for success in the corporate world.

One of the skills I learned was writing and speaking in the local language in just two months, which was essential to excel in my performance there.

Now, whenever I pass through that state and hear people speaking in the local language, I don't feel strange and can easily read each signboard.

I got the opportunity after 25 years to work in that state again; this time, I was fluent.

Later on, I got an excellent job opportunity in a multinational company with all the luxury facilities that I had never availed earlier, so I left my first organization with all thanks to all the people for their support during my difficult time, and I set off on a new journey to a new place, new people, new technology, new challenges, and new learning.

The Moral of a Story

"Success always follows only after a bunch of failures. Successful people never give up and love rough weather and bad roads because this guarantees success."

Chapter 10

Share Market > A Funny Game

"I will tell you how to become rich. Close the door. Be fearful when others are greedy. Be greedy when others are fearful".
Warren Buffett

Courtesy: Image source Share market: India.com

In this world, change is the untold truth. We develop new technology, science, politics, and social or financial updates daily.

There is dynamic balancing around the world in the best interest of everyone.

No one wants to be at a standstill but continuously keep themselves moving.

Life is full of races, everyone is running in this race and wants to be a winner, and their objectives may differ.

If anyone can do why can't I, I also don't want to be a loser.

There is a famous saying, "Winner never quits, and a quitter never wins," so was I; how could I so easily quit without participating in this global race?

I was mature and could decide independently; there was no need to see what others were doing. I had to find my path of happiness & prosperity in life, and I had to achieve this in the shortest period.

Good health and good wealth are the benchmark of any successful person.

I was dreaming the same, but poor financial condition was the main hurdle, and the path to success was full of obstacles.

For a successful person, money is one of the predominant factors.

My friend, good luck and bad luck, were again looking towards me with some optimistic hope as they didn't find any exciting thing to do for so many days, and their life was turning boring, so they were me.

Everyone wants to do some challenging and adventurous things; you can't live long with tasteless food or tasteless life.

We decided to go on another adventurous journey.

Would you like to ride with us on this journey once again? Let's move and have an amusement.

The dynamics of the market change every day, in fact, every hour. The market is very volatile, and overall global market sentiments govern it.

The share market index is one of the barometers for monitoring the success and failure of any company.

A reasonable and rising share price indicates the growth of the company, and based on the performance, investor plan to invest in that particular company on the prediction of long sustainable development.

It is not a regression analysis graph showing continual share price growth.

In statistical analysis, you can't predict the accuracy based on data only.

The accuracy and authenticity of the data are of prime importance.

Playing in the share market is a gambling game because your decisions depend on many hypothetical models, theories, and market sentiments.

It is optional that your prediction always works well; it is often vice versa.

Everyone thinks this is the shortest route to becoming a billionaire in a concise period.

In this field, there is no grading of the intensity of the knowledge, even if you may think you are an expert.

On any day, there may be money rain, or you can say the flood of money, and the very next day, it may desert and wipe out your whole money.

In this field, many players play underground games that no one can easily understand.

As a young salary-paid employee, I started dreaming that only salary couldn't fulfill my dreams.

Success combines meticulous planning, hard work, good knowledge, and good luck.

Peoples say luck favors the brave. I also started thinking in this direction to become one of the most courageous people in the share market because luck will favor me; at the other corner, lousy luck was standing, smiling, and thinking, this time, it was his turn.

Saving that I had earned from my tiny salary always attracted me to do some short-time adventures to become financially independent, get settled, and live a leisurely life for the rest of my age.

I started dreaming, sitting outside the swimming pool, reading the newspaper on the share market with a cup of cold coffee with a beautiful family at the overseas picnic spot.

In my company, I have seen many people spend most of their office time in detailed discussions on this topic, mostly related to different companies' performance and future growth plans.

I was a new entrant in this field and was very excited to be part of this, so I was silently used to hearing their discussion and learning the technical concepts of this subject.

After a few months of self-learning training sessions, those were my hidden coach, as I didn't take any formal training from them.

There is a famous proverb that quacks are dangerous.

The same happened to me; I had declared and certified myself as the subject expert, but no one knew.

I was a new entrant baby fish in the giant share market ocean. There were millions of fish of all sizes in the sea.

Once you start feeling like this, you start making your own decision, which may lead to a financial fatal.

One day, I invested my hard-earned money in purchasing one of the company shares.

I planned a strategy on my own that I should go for the branded blue chip company; I thought that premium company shares would give a premium return.

After proper registration, I visited one local share broker and consultant nearby.

Rather than advising anything, he had consented to my idea and was immediately ready to process hard-earned money for purchasing shares at a very premium rate.

I did not doubt his capability because he used to manage the funds of many high-salaried employees of our company. He was a reputed big experienced person in this market.

It had given enormous booster confidence to me.

I felt myself one of the luckiest people on this earth, and I started believing to be the top wealth holder as per the theory of the law of attraction.

No one can understand or predict a game of luck.

Growth was slow, and study and share prices started to rise. Another task I assigned myself for going daily to a library, reading the newspapers, and checking share price trends.

Along with me, many big players were used to daily visit the library to do the data study and plan for the next day's strategy.

In those days, people of different age groups of mixed genders visited the library to enhance their knowledge of various subjects.

Along with the study, this was a short-time social gathering too.

Since childhood, I was a regular visitor to the library, so it was my fun time too.

Whenever I used to see the share market column in the newspaper, the experienced people of the share market sitting around used to look at me, but they never said anything.

After a month, the share price started declining; it was new to me. I was very optimistic that this was a minor correction the price would go up again.

In a week, the declining rate became very fast, and within two months, I'd lost almost 90 % of my investment; this was just like a one-atom bomb dropped over you.

It was difficult for me to react. I was very helpless; no one was there to guide or support me.

In a very short time, I lost my 100 % money.

It did not happen with me alone, but everyone those experienced persons were the great sufferer.

The bad news started to surface in the newspapers that one of the stock exchange-based share market brokers had done a scam; by opening a fake company, people invested millions of dollars in those companies and finally drowned.

It was the rarest biggest scam in the history of the share market.

Share brokers run away with fraudulent money.

I was one of the tiny fish victims of the share market.

Once again, bad luck shattered my billionaire dream. He was continuously smiling over me.

I was back to square with zero saving balance to start a new journey again.

I lost everything. It was a small story, but it gave a big lesson to me.

The Moral of a Story

"You should have big dreams and should work to accomplish them. History is full of such successful people who started from scratch, but in the end, they were global celebrities. They were successful because they planned everything meticulously, implemented, and worked till perfection or you can say till excellence if it is not perfect."

Chapter 11

First Foreign Tour> Am I Really Lucky?

"No one realizes how beautiful it is to travel until he comes home and rests his head on his old, familiar pillow."

Lin Yutang, a Chinese Novelist and philosopher

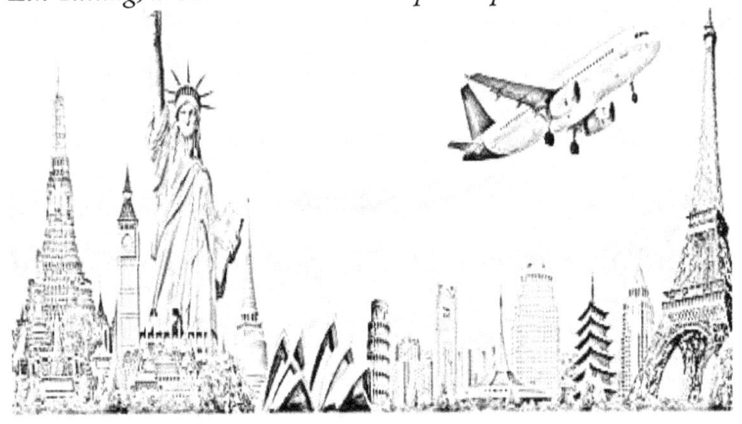

Courtesy: Foreign tour: Image for representation only

In my earlier story, I told about many firsts. Everyone loves their country too much but gets excited once they can explore the outside world.

It is everyone's dream to travel overseas, whether personal or official, at least once in their lifetime.

Overseas travels open the door to interacting with different cultures, people, languages, foods, etc.

I was not different from others; in those days, if someone visited another country, it was considered a very prestigious event; it is just like when a person from a small village visited a big city for the first time and shared their experience with people around him.

As shared earlier, it happened once in my childhood when two friends returned from a similar journey.

I also had a dream to travel once in a lifetime to an overseas country.

At that time, I worked in a multinational company and had already completed five years there.

Our company was not only a multinational at the same time, it was also a diversified business company.

Due to diversification, they used to expand their capacity across the globe for better business prospects.

One of the strategies was to arrange internal resources for a new project, which met the two objectives; the first was to provide opportunities for their employee's growth as well as the organization a pool of multitasking people.

For one such expansion project, there was a need for two people from our unit.

In my company, there were a bunch of more than fifty eligible engineers who had indirectly produced their candidature for this project in

Thailand. It was a lifetime opportunity for anyone in those days to make them financially strong and have significant social recognition.

Our company Sr. Executive president had to decide and pick up only two engineers from this pool. Most of the people were higher in seniority than me.

In my first organization, as a protocol, I gave a whole day report to him on every night shift duty as and when I was on the night shift.

This task was very challenging, as I had to keep updated with the whole day's reports with all micro details and explanations for any deviation if I was reporting to him in only two-minute time. You can call it an exact report.

He was a very brilliant and sharp observer with technical engineering calculations on his fingertip.

One of his best qualities was recognizing each individual with his voice over the phone. I was also one of them.

During my reporting to him, I used to prepare a full-day report very meticulously, which impressed him a lot; another beauty of the report was complete transparency with no hidden information and agenda that he liked very much.

My presentation quality helped him to make up his mind to finalize the first candidate for that overseas project.

On a beautiful day, his executive assistant called my immediate reporting manager's office and said the boss was calling me immediately.

Another beauty of our senior executive president was his fast decision-making skill.

In those days, visiting his office was a big thing for a junior person in rank.

As soon as I got communication to reach there immediately, I was feared and sweating, my heart started bumping and heartbeats very high.

I had no idea at all that what would be happening next moment with me.

Such a situation often arises in people's life.

I started praying to god, what shall I do if something wrong happened to me and if they punished me?

There was dark around me because no one knew what would be next.

Those were winter days, my colleagues wore full woolen clothes, and I was sweating even without winter cloth; time was full of anxiety.

Lastly, I first reached his executive assistant's office and asked about his calling to me.

He told you to go to the boss's cabin and meet him immediately.

Full of fear and anxiety in my mind, I entered his office because he spoke very little and to the point.

I stood with both hands folded before him.

He did not say a single word, directly came to the point, and asked me a one-line question; the answer should be either yes or no.

He straight forward asked me are you interested in the Thailand project.

I was silent for a few seconds; I couldn't believe it, and soon I realized I had to answer him.

With all internal pleasure, I said, yes, I am.

He said ok, you can go.

I felt fortunate; my dream was coming true as there was a complete chance to get a permanent appointment to work there if my performance was satisfactory.

Once again, festival moments and happiness were in everyone's eyes.

Was I really lucky?

It may be others' envy, but it was my pride.

Immediately I started getting VIP treatment from my colleagues and reporting manager; earlier, it was not the case.

I got an excellent performance appraisal rating and an outstanding increment that year.

If you have a good friend to help you, you will also have people to pull your leg.

It is a universal truth that no one can deny.

One of my senior colleagues approached him to present his strong candidature.

Once again, I thought my good luck was not long-lasting and shall be turned into bad luck again.

Boss returned him empty-handed with one strong message: I was qualified for this project, and he was overqualified.

We can learn the diplomatic message communication skill here to satisfy everyone.

I retained my overseas trip seat and also had good luck.

Nowadays, it is effortless to go overseas, and no one bothers or notices about this.

Finally, I got my first passport, first visa, and at the same time, my fiancé.

She is now my lovely wife.

How did life change in just a few months? Could you think?

My friend, good luck, was this time in a jubilant mood.

When luck favors them, a talented unfortunate bachelor suddenly becomes the talk of the town in his social, professional, and personal life.

Immediately before leaving, I got engaged; it happened so fast that I'd never thought about this.

With a concise loving memory of my fiancé and my loving friends, I had left for the unseen memorable journey that was Thailand.

It is a fantastic experience when you first time sees from a plane a beautiful lovely earth; it seems like you wear golden and diamond jewelry at night and lovely green in the morning, surrounded by water and the infinite Universe, and realize that you are a tiny entity on this earth.

You are nothing in this immense Universe.

Finally, I landed on a new foreign soil with a new dream, new life, and loving memories of all my close friends and relatives, and to be life partners.

There was a warm welcome to me at the new place by our new colleagues.

There was an exciting experience on day one when we went out into the market to purchase some daily wear, we tried our best to explain our needs, but even after half an hour, we couldn't explain our requirements to the shop owner.

It was a comedy situation to explain with different body language but failed attempt.

Finally, we called upon the cab driver to get the desired item.

Sometimes language is the biggest constraint, and how it is difficult to manage due to a lack of proper communication media or sources.

Immediately I purchased one language dictionary from English to Thai; later on, this became a blockbuster for me to communicate with all local people easily.

From the very next day, there were three holidays. Our team decided to visit Pattaya Beach and have some fun.

We all landed on a lovely designed ship; everyone enjoyed Thai music and dancing, it was total entertainment, and finally, we reached there in time.

We were a total of six people.

In Thailand, water sport is trendy at beaches.

One of the water sports is Banana air balloon drive. In this drive, four to five persons can sit on an air balloon in a banana shape and connect with a boat.

We decided to go for that; the boat rider was taking us into the deep sea, which was a thrilling experience for all of us. It was our first adventure, and we had given the challenge to the mighty ocean.

We all were enjoying our banana air balloon ride and feeling thrilled.

After fifteen minutes of driving, we were in the deep sea, there was only water, and you didn't know the depth of it.

One of my friends was sitting with a boat rider and guiding him.

Within a second, suddenly boat driver took a U-turn. All of us were thinking that it would be a routine drive.

The language was a significant constraint for communication; he could understand only fractured English.

Due to a sudden turn, we all three fell into the sea; we were unprepared for that and started shouting for our survival.

The boat driver explained in Thai, but we were helpless.

Death was before us, and we were about to disappear into the deep sea.

There was a fight between good and bad luck.

Good luck was crying, but bad luck had a secret smile on our faces.

In a fraction of a second, we all acknowledged that today was our last day, started praying to god for any possible miracle, and remembered all our loved ones.

I was recently engaged last week, and I felt sad for my fiancé that due to this, I'll leave everyone crying forever.

My friend, sitting in a boat, told us there was no need to worry; you would never drown.

To our surprise, we all were still floating, but there was a big shocked situation for all of us.

We had firmly caught hold of the boat; you might be thinking how it happened, are everyone knows the swimming.

It was not the case; no one knew the swimming.

Our friend informed us that we were wearing the life jacket that had helped us to float on the sea.

The very first time, we came to understand the importance of a life jacket; it may be funny, and you will laugh but understand a weak heart person could die due to this adverse significant impact of lack of awareness.

Once loaded in the boat for our return journey, we learned it was a part of the game, played routinely with each air balloon banana rider for their adventurous amusement.

Now, whenever I remember that banana drive, I still get scared.

It was a fascinating journey, but later on, we couldn't find the opportunity for the second trip.

Later, we visited many beautiful local places during our stay and interacted with many people to understand the country's culture.

It was a fantastic experience.

Within a few days, I learned that our sister organization was planning to retain all of us in Thailand as permanent employees.

That was a double bonanza for me; once again, I started daydreaming with all my wish lists for my plan in Thailand.

In such a moment, you can't hide the level of happiness, but no one knows how good weather turns into bad weather in a short period.

I could have realized that this is the cycle of bad and good.

In 1997, there was a large-scale money depreciation in South East Asian countries.

It had a massive impact, especially in a country like Thailand.

The currency of transactions for this project was in Dollars; due to the devaluation of the Thai Baht (Thai currency), project costs also increased very high.

The company had to mitigate this impact immediately by bringing down project costs.

The most straightforward target and action plan was to cut down overhead costs.

In any business, this is the first step an organization takes.

The very first action they took; they had dropped the idea of hiring four additional engineers who were on deputation; I was one of them.

Our dream became a nightmare for all of us.

We had to return to our respective plants within a short period.

Destiny played its role beautifully; we were helpless, poor guys with no alternative but to return.

Our good luck was short-lasting this time, but bad luck replaced this.

Could you imagine that this happened only once in the history of Thailand, and it never occurred later on?

I could not think, and even not dared to ask that superpower, why it happened only to me.

Later on, I traveled to many countries.

The Moral of a Story

"Destiny always had a life plan for every individual, and accordingly, we act, and other people work; you can't dictate to him; you have only to obey him."

Chapter 12

To Settle in USA > Day or Night Dreaming
"The American dream belongs to all of us."
Kamala Harris, Vice President USA

Settle in the USA: Image for representation only.

Sound sleep is the best process for rejuvenating our body, repairing damaged cells, and getting our body ready for the next day's activities.

After a long sleep, we do feel refreshed and energetic.

Some people sleep in the daytime. Also, that only sounds good once and if you are ill and recommended by a Doctor to do so.

One thing is evident when you are in a deep sleep and disconnected from the outer world; you immediately connect with your inner subconscious world.

Your thought turns into dreams and appears accordingly.

Dreams are dreams. You can see dreams whether you sleep day or night, but how much these are close to reality, we can't say.

There are two types of dreamers, night dreamers and day-dreamers.

The subconscious mind controls night dreamers, and the conscious mind governs daydreamers.

There is a high probability for the success of daydreamers; although it is not a hundred percent sure to succeed, this is only sometimes the case with night dreamers.

Successful in the world are persons who have thought beyond others' imagination and achieved their ambitions.

It is the rights of everyone to be ambitious; the same applies to me.

As an engineer, I was ambitious to succeed in my field.

Sometimes you have induced ambition means internally, you would like to fulfill these dreams and work according to that.

Sometimes you have been forced to do that, but internally, you are not ready; this is called forced ambition.

This time, I was in the second category because I had no choice but to accept to do.

My wife's elder brother is working in the US, and he had advised me to do some software-related courses and asked me to come down to the US, as there were ample opportunities to build my carrier exponentially. Per him, there will be a rain of dollars compared to your local currency based on your available skills.

The offer was very lucrative, and in those days, settling in the US was a dream for most people; although this was not my dream, this time, my wife was looking as a daydreamer.

To fulfill this forced ambition, I have to spend quality time doing quality courses in software languages like C, C++, Java, DBMS (Data Base Management System), etc. These were in significant demand in those days.

I had basic computer programming knowledge from my earlier experience.

Based on his input, during that time, Hyderabad (India) was one of the most convenient and cheapest places to do these courses.

The problem was that I was on the job, and getting at least six months' unpaid leave from the organization took a lot of work.

No management afford to release their bright employees for self-study; it never happened in the history of that organization.

It was an impossible task, but if you have decided to move forward, ways will automatically come before you and guide you to get it done.

I immediately approached my immediate boss.

Unfortunately, he was not a computer-savvy man; he didn't understand my out of box idea and, as per routine management practice, rudely returned me with a big NO.

It was an expected outcome in any organization. Emotion can't supersede professionalism.

Bad Luck shared a big smile and then laughed when I was coming out of his office. Good Luck was a little bit not confident with this move.

I was nervous, but slowly, he kept his hand over my shoulder, looked towards me, and shook his head positively to raise my confidence.

US President Mr. Abraham Lincoln once said, "If friendship is your weakest point, then you are the strongest person in the world." I was feeling the same.

Good Luck was always supportive of me. He murmured in my ear and gave me some tips.

I was well aware, now where to approach to get the green signal; checking with reporting boss was to ensure that in the future, he should not have an option of saying no for not approaching him.

There is a saying in management that you should not stand in front of your boss and behind the horse because both will kick you out when you are extra clever.

Since he had said no, I immediately rushed to my favorite CEO, who once gave me the opportunity for my first overseas travel.

I talked and shared my idea that I would need a six-month unpaid study leave for higher-level study and better opportunities in the IT field.

As I shared with you in my earlier story, my CEO was famous for his instant decision-making skills and extraordinarily advanced thinking, and he was well aware of my computer programing skill.

He immediately sanctioned my leave and gave all the best blessings for my prospects ahead.

Very few lucky people get such an excellent super boss. It is a rare phenomenon globally.

I missed mentioning that my wife was also part of this journey, which means we were simultaneously planning for the same course.

As soon as this news spread all around the corner, people could not believe that for a person like me who is working at this junior level, CEO had approved my leave for study.

There was no direct benefit to the organization by doing so.

Luck favors brave, so was happened to me, but it was a defeat to my immediate boss; he could not believe that a miracle was possible without his consent.

He was furious about my act, approached the CEO, and tried to use his authority to cancel my sanctioned leave.

Bad Luck and Good Luck immensely enjoyed this incident with me this time.

You might think that bad Luck always creates problems, but my friend, you should know that every criticism is the next ladder of success.

I firmly believe that you can excel in your performance in the odd situation, making you stronger.

No one can defeat you and your ambition if God is with you.

The same happened to me. CEO told his philosophy to my boss that there are two sides of the coin.

The first side is that if he leaves the organization for his future, we should not be an obstacle in his path; secondly, if he, after completion of his course, did not get a good opportunity, then after his return, I will be the valuable asset to the organization, and add value to the organization because CEO was computer savvy.

He evaluated this skill when I developed Excel software for my department without external support.

That software, after so many years still running in the organization.

The CEO's answer was so perfect, he was answerless and returned to his office without uttering a single word. Good Luck, as usual, had the blessing for me with a big thump up.

He could easily mark pleasure on my face.

You can hide your sorrow, but it is challenging for happiness.

Many muscles work together in a team to bring a lovely smile to your face, but this is not the case with sorrow.

My immediate boss, who was a very diplomatic person, was defeated by my simplicity.

Simplicity is the biggest weapon to become successful.

Diplomacy failed, and ambition won the game and cleared the first hurdle.

It was the time of Oct '20, and I had to arrange the fund to get admission to the best-reputed software coaching classes for these courses.

It was an adamant and challenging time due to the availability of minimal financial resources with no income for the next six to eight months.

Finally, we landed in Hyderabad with the support of our close friend; he provided all resources for our comfortable stay there.

I was not used to their regional language, only my wife was fluent because she was born and brought up there, but that was not a significant challenge for us.

We got admission to the well-reputed coaching center in the city and started another journey with the highest level of energy, excitement, and many big plans ahead.

One of the plans was to have an excellent job for both of us and have an expanded family in the US only, with US citizenship for all.

It was our well-planned task, the only thing before us was a six-month long time, and we had to finish every related course within this stipulated period.

We both had the added advantage of past good computer programming knowledge.

Everything was going well and running according to our planning; we were on the seventh sky.

Just after a month, the pleasant weather started turning turbulent; it was like you were on a flight flying smoothly, and suddenly, black thunder started storming the flight with many ups and downs. Still, a skilled pilot controlled the plane and escaped this unpleasant weather.

The beautiful blue sky turned blackish with unexpected high-velocity wind flow to deviate our path.

Unpleasant news started airing in the sky about the poor performance of the dot com IT companies in Silicon Valley.

It was the first sign of discomfort; like a skilled pilot, we thought bad weather would soon pass, and everything would be alright.

Day and night, we worked very hard to enhance our skills in preplanned scheduled time, compromising all our leisure time and life.

During this period as a stress buster, we have attended a couple of social trips to nearby holy places and enjoyed a couple of movies with the courtesy of close friends and their next chain of friend circles.

Since I was uncomfortable with the local language, it was a fun time, too, to learn a few words and manage the show.

Language and food was a big challenge to me.

Time passed, and the fund was also drying; although it wasn't a sign of desert, the level was going down, although we had fine-tuned our expenses to the optimum level.

In those days, we had learned a corporate lesson of survival of the fittest.

We were the best fund manager to manage every penny of money for the best utilization to meet our routine and academic expenses.

We had meticulously planned our expenses for approximately six to seven months, with a certain amount kept aside for our returned journey.

Every new challenge teaches you a big lesson, and we learn new technical and life lessons daily.

The situation was getting worse in the US as dot com companies' balloons started bursting soon.

One by one, Silicon Valley companies failed to withstand themselves there.

Fear and anxiety started appearing on our faces now; this was the time when in the next two months, we were about to finish all our courses.

It is seldom happening that things happen according to your plan.

One more bad news arrived, I had lost my inspiring, loving father.

I had to leave my classes and return home, and after completing all rituals in the next ten days, I went back to attend my remaining courses.

Now news across the country flashes like lightning that thousands of people are jobless due to Dot Com failure in the US.

Most companies show their employees the exit door, ask them to leave immediately and look for other opportunities.

It wasn't a healthy sign; since no similar skill jobs were there, people started returning to their respective home countries.

Now there was only dark in front of us. We didn't understand anything.

My wife's brother shared the final bad news that the situation was terrible, and we had no hope.

We got entirely shattered. All our efforts and investment became guttered; we were a helpless newly married couple.

The only thing that was very clear was destiny is not in your hand; you are the only actor playing their role on the world drama stage.

You can't challenge the almighty's decision. You only have to accept them.

Another bad news was waiting for me after this sad story; there was an untimely death of my CEO.

Good fortune turned into lousy Luck.

I was aware of my future, but now there will be no godfather at my current organization; I will have to fight myself only; no one will care about me.

Before me, there will be hundreds of financial, social, personal, and professional challenges.

Once again, I have to start from scratch.

With the last money saved for our return journey, we packed up our luggage, even though we did not have the money to have some snacks with us, and left the place with tears in our eyes and two dollars to pay our coolie charges at our hometown railway station.

Bad Luck had a great smile; suddenly, he had looked towards Good Luck, whose face was flat and expressionless.

Bad Luck won this battle after the journey of many peaks and valleys on a smooth, rough road.

Life is lovely, showing every color in different phases of time.

Once again, we started a new journey with new hope, new expectation, and new energy, as you can't stand still by carrying your past bad experiences.

Again our life was waiting for a new destination with new good and bad experiences.

I hope you have very much enjoyed this extraordinary life story.

The Moral of a Story

"In every odd situation, maintain your patience; turbulence is about to come, but it can't demolish you. There is sunlight after every night. It is the universal truth, and no one can deny this. Let's enjoy every moment of life and thank God because we do not know what big he has planned for us".

Chapter 13

New Home > Who Is the Great Financial Planner?

"A house is made with walls and beams; a home with love and dreams."
Ralph Waldo Emerson

New home: Image for representation only

Rented house or my home, which one is better?

Please differentiate between house and home. I hope yes.

Still, I would like to share the difference; with the house; the first thought that comes to our mind, a structure is built with bricks, sand, cement, water, some combinations of color, and furniture.

When we think about home, the first thought that comes into our mind is a relationship that binds a whole family, having a lot of emotions, memories, and connectivity among all family members.

It doesn't count bricks or the physical condition of the house.

A home is another word for the love and affection of a family.

In a child's words, a "FAMILY" could be defined as "Father and Mother, I love You."

As per the Britannica dictionary, a building made for people or a family is known as a house. The family living in a house is known as a home.

There is a vast difference between these two terms.

If I ask you which one you would like, it would be home, or you can say my dream home.

Many people live in the house, and many lives in the home.

Home brings long-lasting belongingness.

I had spent most of my early life in a house made up of bricks only. I dreamed of having a home, but financial conditions never supported me in fulfilling this ambition.

As mentioned earlier, God favors braves, and if you have decided to do something better in your life, opportunity follows the route of your ambition.

At the age of 34, I'd decided to have my own home; that time, I had hardly a penny in my pocket.

It was a big dream and a challenging task with a single small source of earnings.

Once again discussion process has been started in the family.

In modern management terminology, you can make a decision using the famous "Force field analysis" tool. In this tool, you have two options, first, driving force, and second, restraining influence.

You can decide based on a higher score on either side.

In this exercise, based on a higher score on the driving force side, we decided to go for the dream home option.

An extensive, complicated process of acquiring a home loan was started, with no guarantee except the new home.

That is why all banks offer this as a home loan, not a house loan.

You can understand how the bank captures your sentiments and connects with you for a long duration, like twenty years, that covers at least three generations.

Although I had managed to get the home loan, my dream home.

I planned to keep the home ready for stay only, not to rent out, but soon, I realized it would not be financially possible to keep it vacant as I'd found one tenant to begin the journey of a second source of income to manage loan EMIs.

It was the first time I had a second source of earnings, and loan EMI was managing well for the following year.

Happy days could not last longer; shortly, tenants started reluctance to pay monthly rent, financial trouble started mounting, and it became difficult to manage the EMI.

At the crucial moment, with the grace of God, I received a handsome salary increment and organized the show.

I immediately asked the tenant to vacate the house and looked for a second tenant.

It may seem to be a boring story, but there are moments when you are helpless and find yourself in a vicious circle, and suddenly, you receive some surprising financial support that you can't imagine.

The new tenant was a farmer and had a good earning to pay my small rent. It was tiny money for him.

A few months, as usual, were ok, but once again same trouble started of inconsistent receiving rent; suddenly, a financial crisis started for him.

I was amazed that both the tenant was a businessman and were in very healthy financial conditions, and both the time after completion of one year, they became financially unstable.

The same was again happening to me, another big challenge.

I couldn't believe that it was a coincidence or something else. Phenomena were the same for both the tenants but unbelievable.

I was under tremendous financial stress then, and no way around there.

This time, bad luck was continually smiling over good luck and tirelessly making fun of my situation.

There is a saying that if no one is with you, at least some superpower is always there to help you.

I don't know how, but suddenly, a miracle happened; within a week, I got an excellent job offer with an excellent salary, position, and relocation opportunity in a nearby big city.

I had been trying for more than three years.

It was a different assignment as corporate head of quality in a big multinational business group. You could call it a dream job.

Once again, I'd overcome the financial problem, and life was on a regular track.

Don't you think this is a game of bad and good luck, and I was the luckiest one every time?

In a year, I'd purchased one piece of land and, the very next year, decided to sell this house due to frequent financial challenges, and purchase a new house, pardoning me technically; it was my first home at my current location.

It was my first home because my younger son arrived in this world in this home only, and we became a complete family here.

Can you imagine a feeling of a great family; we have started a new journey here.

Meanwhile, the new tenant purchased the house with the commitment to paying the total amount in the next three months.

A few months later, the same trouble started inconsistent receiving rent; suddenly, a financial crisis started for him, and he repeatedly extended his payment duration to finish the deal.

Pressure started building on me to pay the EMI of my new home, land, and old house.

I needed help with arranging the fund to manage my day-to-day expenses.

There was a good salary but a negative bank balance with other expenses and expenses related to growing kids.

The whole financial planning failed, and this period continued for the next two years.

You can imagine the situation. We were passing through one of the scary situations.

But God is great, and no one can challenge his extraordinary advanced planning that no one can even understand.

He has future planning for an unlimited period in his superpower advanced computer system that is beyond the understanding of a human being.

As humans, we hardly use a tiny percentage of our brains; you can imagine how big he is, the perfect planner of the universe.

When I was facing my life's worst financial challenge, a new hope ray entered this scenario; a new source of funds arrived to help me out, and old investments started getting matured during that period only; those invested many years back at the start of my carrier, and I'd never thought but thanked God for his ultimate timing to get me out from this bad phase.

I learned a big corporate lesson: you have to ensure financial security when you are going on an adventurous tour of finance.

I was lucky to be able to manage that lousy show.

Finally, I got the total amount from my buyer in the next two years and got a handsome return from selling land to pay off my home loan concisely.

The loan tenure was for 20 years, but I repaid the loan next five years only.

Later on, I purchased one more home and, at the same time, got another job change opportunity with a significant salary rise and outstanding designation in another location.

I'd pay the loan in the next five years.

Once I'd paid both loans, I got job opportunities in my hometown again, and

I shifted to my dream house where my kids were born and brought up.

We now enjoy every moment we live to date in our dream home.

At the beginning of this chapter, the photo is of my dream house.

Why did I choose this chapter as number 13? Because my home's lucky number is 13?

What would you say about this story? How much would you rate this?

Now, when I remember my tough days, I only close my eyes and thank God and think whether it was bad luck or good luck because now I am financially secure and living a comfortable life.

The Moral of a Story

"Everyone thinks that they are good financial planners. Big corporate house hires financial experts for their business; those are highly qualified from top reputed financial institutes, but the greatest financial planner is the almighty superpower who takes care of everyone's balance sheet very accurately with no flaw and the highest sigma level in the statistical calculation of this number is beyond the capability of highest ranked computer in the world".

Chapter 14

My First Car Drive> Driving for Life after Life

"The way I drive, the way I handle a car, is an expression of my inner feelings."

Lewis Hamilton, A formula One driver

My first car drive: Image for representation only

In the management lesson of Maslow's theory of satisfaction, need and expectation starts from the basics of food, shelter, and cloth that reach the highest level of self-actualization.

Most people on this earth pass through this cycle, as this is a natural human tendency to be recognized by others to satisfy their self-esteem.

There is an extensive wish list for an individual, and they run behind them to fulfill throughout their life cycle, and at the end, they are surprised to see that they have achieved nothing.

I am among those billions of self-esteemed aspirants who want to be socially recognized.

In the social recognition process, one of the most important things you should have is the luxuries that others either do not afford to have or are not able to meet the benchmark you have set in the society you are living in.

It is a tendency of mine, too; if you have, then why don't I have?

It is invisible competition among ourselves.

I was not a poor guy alone, entangled in this vicious circle in which there is one-way traffic; you can only enter but difficult or no way to come out.

The beauty of this psychological journey is that everyone wants to be a traveler at any cost; no one can stop you when once it is decided.

The same happened in my happy family life, running smoothly without many hurdles.

Despite having limited financial resources, I felt lucky to have such a wonderful life.

On a beautiful evening, I returned from the office and had tea and snacks with my Wife and lovely son on the balcony.

My Wife was eagerly awaiting my return; she asked me to look down from my third-floor flat on the street to look at a new car purchased by one of my colleagues.

The vehicle was adequately covered and attracted the attention of many people passing nearby.

There was a big optimistic smile on her face, her eyes were telling the Story, her body was full of energy, and her expectation was at the highest level; there was not a single word of communication between us, and thoughts were getting exchanged without the support of communication media.

It was sufficient time for me to get the situation to understand and respond accordingly.

The financial storm was about to tap my door, but I could realize the sound of steps from long away coming towards me.

They successfully communicated what they wanted to do; it was my turn to take the well-calculated risk to say yes or no.

You may call it telepathy.

In a family matter, you can't be straightforward; your EQ (Emotional Quotient) level is very high, and you must manage it well, else side effects are long-lasting, like an arrow shot from a bow never returning similarly spoken words.

Only your communication skill using diplomatic words could do the wonder.

I took a strategic pause; like in sports, there is time to revise the game plan.

Both of them were silently looking towards me optimistically.

During this pause, I quickly calculated the financial impact by maintaining sufficient liquidity to manage the daily and contingency expenses.

Time was very short. I had to decide in a very fraction of a second, but I took a long pause.

They suddenly fired a question over me when a long pause was extending beyond their tolerance, what is your decision?

Life is so beautiful that it tests you in every situation.

Both my good and bad luck friends were confused and were in a dilemma about how good and bad decisions could impact them; they were silent and observing me, and I realized that no one could do this.

Finally, with my quick calculation, I decided to proceed with this project.

Our family had a triumphant moment as this was the first car in our extended family.

Not to overextend this Story, we had approached the Bank to finance the car; I got approval, and the day came to purchase our dream car.

Since both did not have driving licenses, my close friend helped us to drive and bring the car by traveling around 100 + kilometers from the showroom.

It was a beautiful black car, our favorite color; soon, we hired a trainer to teach us the driving basics of the vehicle. In a week, we had a learning license.

We were living in a big company, green-lustered campus surrounded by beautiful big trees and concrete roads, and along the road, there was an unprotected storm water sloppy drainage trench.

Overall it was a lovely township with all amenities, everyone would like to live there, and the best place for a sound retirement life, but unfortunately, you can't stay after retirement.

It was a double bonanza for us; now we were going to take a ride in this beautiful township, you know; black color attracts very quickly to everyone.

It was the first black car in the township.

My Wife was highly excited to take the first ride in the colony that might impress others known to us. It was just like a neighbor's envy but an owner's pride.

In the evening, after getting a learning license, she was ready to start; I could see a moment of joy on her face.

She had tried to hide the happiness, but this was a natural phenomenon, and she couldn't restrict herself.

A million-dollar smile was on her face.

The first challenge was waiting for her; a big buffalo was sitting on the road, and it wasn't easy to get rid of her.

She had decided to take a left turn to save the buffalo; during the activity, due to poor steering control, the car started to ram down toward the storm water drainage trench line almost four feet below the main road.

The car was almost to get overturned; suddenly, I applied the hand brake and stopped the car to go down further.

We were saved by a fraction of a second.

We were shocked. Our dream car was about to become part of a garbage collection store.

It was a big challenge to bring the car back on the road. We had called upon an expert driver to help us out.

After a month, I got an excellent job opportunity in a nearby big city, having all facility to live a perfect life there.

This time it was my turn to take the first commercial drive to relocate to our new destination.

The traveling distance was almost 100 kilometers. The Wife was not ready to drive the car due to her last lousy driving experience.

Before this drive, I took a small test drive to acclimate to various car functions.

The biggest challenge was facing a big vehicle coming from the other side due to two lane road with no clear bifurcation. It was not a highway.

As and when I used to see any vehicle coming from the other side, my hands used to start shivering on the steering wheel.

It was our first evening drive for three hours.

I'd smoothly covered around seventy kilometers without hassle; it was a rainy thunder evening.

I was driving first time in the most challenging situation.

Heavy rains were pouring on the car along with thunder, and the wind was creating difficulty there; it was almost not possible to drive the vehicle with minimal distance visibility.

Road was two lanes only, and there was no bifurcation for proper guidance to the opposite direction running vehicle.

As a driver, you were the best judge of your driving skill; it was just like a live streaming of your talent.

You were entirely dependent on the other's skill.

The night was spreading its wing to create the situation more complicated.

No sign of light was on the way; you had to drive the car by your guess.

On that day, vehicle movement was significantly less, and there was no light along the road, creating fear among us.

I was cautiously driving the car, and suddenly, a giant tree fell on the road due to a thunderstorm.

I was driving the car at around 80 kilometers per hour.

I was unprepared, either physically or mentally, to face this situation.

I was scared and, in fear, turned the car steering to the right. We have left side driving system to avoid any accidents.

You can imagine the situation what will be next.

From a very short distance, one vehicle was coming as there was a big blind turn before that, so you can't judge the car's proximity due to poor visibility.

The car turned to the right almost by ninety degrees, and I saw that one car was coming from the opposite side, and our vehicle was also on the same side; immediately, in a fraction of a second, I'd fully turned steering to the left side. The car was about to turn upside down.

I did not know who was winning the race this time, my good luck or bad luck; I had purchased the car since then, and both were fully confused. No one was laughing this time.

Both had full sympathy for us; both wanted to see us alive.

The first thought that came into my mind was that we had finished, and this was the end of the Story of this beautiful life; we were about to leave this world in a moment and get set go for a new journey that no one knew.

Old peoples say, and also somewhere mentioned in the holy books, that people take new life and are born with fixed numbers of breath, and once you complete your quota of breath, you have to go back.

All three completed the quota of breaths, and the time had come to say goodbye to all.

Unfortunately, no one was there to say bye to us.

Magic is magic; it is not the hand skill of a magician who shows us many beautiful tricks.

It is the most prominent magician of the universe, who controls everything, and we have to act according to that.

Magic happened; a car about to turn fully upside down followed the science theory of tangential force $= mv2/r$, and with a very sharp margin center of gravity of the vehicle shifted towards the right, and the car got balanced with all four wheels.

There was not a single minor injury to us.

We were safe, thanked almighty once again for his timely presence, took everything in his control, and finished the saving of lives with micro-level accuracy.

Statistically, it was the highest six sigma level, where the fatality rate is almost nil in billions of cases.

Since I am a certified six sigma black belt, I can understand the importance of this number.

Last but not least, both my good and bad luck friends were the first time smiling but with complete tears of happiness in their eyes, and there was also a total blessing from both of them; it was a rare incident for them to witness.

Finally, we reached our new destination without much trouble and again started the new journey.

It was another miracle escape, and life started once again.

The Moral of a Story

"Live every moment of your life with family and friends, keep them happy, and spread the love and happiness everywhere, never troubles others for your benefit. Open the account of Blessing and try to credit as much as Blessing possible; you don't know when you will need this fund to meet your emergency requirements."

Chapter 15

Pyramid Scheme > Wants to Be a Billionaire

"I am often asked if Network Marketing is a Pyramid Scheme. My reply is that corporations are Pyramid schemes. A corporation has only one person at the top, generally the CEO, and everyone else below".
Donald Trump

Courtesy: Pyramid scheme: Image for representation only
We know that Egypt's pyramids are world-famous. Tourist from all over the world visits this place and witness the wonder of these creations.

These are the center of attraction for many. There are many rumors spread around the globe about them.

I appreciate the ancient peoples for their intelligence and way ahead in technology to keep the mummies safe for thousands of years.

What I am writing here is not connecting with the subject title.

It's true, but you, once again, imagine the pyramid's design; the design has a top with sharp edges, which means the bottom base is solid, which supports the top, and the overall design is very stable.

Finance is also an important subject that attracts all of us, and everyone does the financial transaction in different modes for different purposes.

Everyday transactions of Billions of dollars take place globally.

For the economy's growth, the flow of funds is essential; it should keep floating to maintain sustainability.

Good liquidity in hand is the backbone of any country, business as well as of family.

The higher the available fund, the higher the stability.

No one wants to be financially unstable; the same was with me.

Earlier, I tried my hands in the share market with disastrous failure.

I was not disturbed by this failure because this failure gave me a lesson that this was not my cup of tea or I was an amateur player of this game with poor or no training on the subject.

I should try something different that no one has done before, and very safe with minimum technical knowledge, and required only interpersonal communication skills.

Contact with people was the key to success; I had to be more social.

In my discussion with many people, I learned that pyramid scheme nowadays is viral, and you are at very minimum risk and low investments.

Still, the return from the plan was highly exponential in a short time compared to the bank's fixed deposit scheme; therein, your invested fund doubled in 8 to10 years.

I got the keys to multiplying the fund multiple times with a one-time investment.

In this scheme, you have to encourage to invest a certain amount of funds to start one channel, and if you want to multiply them in multiple amounts, you can begin to numerous parallel tracks.

Could you imagine money flowing from all directions and pouring over you, like a bath in a big tub filled with cash in a luxurious money room? Isn't it excited us?

As soon as I learned, I immediately started taking a money bath and felt like a billionaire.

The law of attraction always works; whatever you wish, nature will fulfill it.

Believing in these tested facts, I started working on this, and one of my relatives learned that one of the pyramid schemes was doing exceedingly well.

The market was full of advertisements nationwide in all media about that scheme.

I immediately approached him for online registration. I was highly excited at the same time, too, and had a similar dream.

One fine day he came to my house and helped with my online registration, and I'd invested a certain amount of money.

My journey to becoming a billionaire began, but on the other side, my bad friend was smiling and suddenly started laughing over me; this time, he was confident that it was his turn, and he would be the last laughing man.

Since this was a multilayer marketing scheme, you can earn if there is a chain of members below me so that I can enjoy a passive income for a long duration like you write a very successful book or novel that is a globally hit and you are enjoying life extended royalty without much effort.

This book would also be a global blockbuster, but I have put a lot of effort into writing this funny book to reach your hands.

Let's move ahead; it was hardly a day passed; this pyramid scheme got started exposed in social and TV media.

Earlier, it was a promotional advertisement, but this time news started spreading from all corners of the country.

It is human psychology that we want to be pleased with the things that are suited to us or, in other words, favorable to us.

TV and other media were so complacent with this scheme suddenly started behaving differently; news from here and there was spreading like a virus.

You may call it equivalent to Covid-19.

Rumors started about some tricks with this scheme, and chaos started spreading among the people; scheme management immediately came forward to rescue to rebuild the people's confidence.

This scheme consists of filling out online surveys for many clients of this company.

It was the easiest, fastest, and cheapest way of getting the maximum number of opinions of the people, and for that, you get paid.

This scheme was running for the last year, so there was no question of authenticity.

I started getting online surveys from different business profiles as soon as I registered.

I started earning money, and my scheme account got credited.

My best friend, Good Luck, was once again happy because now he was habitual of success; he hardly faced a couple of failures.

He was very confident as well as me too.

Mouthwatering money shortly coming into my pocket was a passive income, and everyone would like to welcome income from this sleeping channel.

In management language, every product has its life cycle, from the growth to the decline phase. It is just like a reverse bathtub curve.

Some products are long-lasting, and some products are premature failure.

No one would like to die before time, and the same was with this scheme; no one can change destiny when the whiteboard is already written with a permanent marker pen.

Shortly adverse news started coming to me from various sources, and my heartbeats which generally follow the healthy adult pattern of 78 beats/min, began to follow the product life cycle of an upward trend.

Can you believe the ideology that some people are always lucky for any family or organization, and others are unlucky?

The same thing was happening to me; as soon as I entered this business, the declining phase started, and shortly after a day, a government agency announced that this was a fraud Ponzi scheme that was making fool millions of people earn a hefty amount.

Sooner, the website became out of reach of users and, through separate media, communicated to all that it was under maintenance.

Many people lost their whole life's hard earnings through this fraud.

I was shocked and speechless; I couldn't believe that my dream to become a billionaire once again shattered as a neat glass gets broken with just a small strike of a hard object, and there remains only a dark background behind this.

I lost my dream like you get to wake up early in the morning from a beautiful dream, and when you open your eyes, you find that life is not always beautiful and realize the reality of the current life challenges, and with new hope again, you start a new day.

My failure adventure added so many life-learning lessons to my life lesson diary.

Oh my god! I forgot to mention; this is the second time my bad friend won, and my good friend lost the battle.

The situation changed; I'd once again tasted defeat. I was defeated. Whom should I blame? Please help me.

The Moral of a Story

"When you enter a new adventure, it is the first step to get detail of all prerequisites, do a SWOT (Strength, Weakness, Opportunity, and Threat), FMEA (Failure Mode Effect Analysis), a market study of a similar type of business model, and last but not least take the expert's opinions, check the depth of river before putting your first leg in the flowing water."

Chapter 16

New Opportunities > Last Minute Change

"Keep away from people who try to belittle your ambitions. Small people always do that, but the great ones make you feel that you too can become great".

Mark Twain, an American writer

New opportunity
last minute change

New opportunity: Image for representation only

Life is full of opportunities; from childhood to our final destination, we come across many betterment opportunities.

We do recognize some of them, and some get elapsed due to a lack of awareness.

An intelligent person knows the trick of grabbing chances and utilizing them fully. Ordinary people wait for the same, so they hardly have incidents where something new comes across them, and by chance, if they get it due to their ignorance, they refuse to accept it.

There is an acceptable difference between success and failure. A successful person is always opportunistic.

They always try to acquire it and take maximum advantage of this, but unsuccessful people fail to do the same and always cry and wait for opportunities to offer on their platter.

In the corporate world, this phenomenon repeatedly occurs like a PDCA (Plan, Do, Check, and Act) improvement cycle.

Here improvement leads to self-improvement.

A person like me always looks to acquire new skills and develop a skill set to survive in this competitive world.

I searched for opportunities to improve my career and still interviewed for a new job.

When you routinely appear for the interview, you can evaluate your market value in the job market.

I've attended many interviews, and this process will continue till I feel that enough is enough and I should quit now and starts living a comfortable, sophisticated life now.

Your success rate in any interview depends on your available skill sets, marketability, meeting the client's requirements, and financial agreement, which is salary.

I was one of the lucky people whose success rate was more than 90 %, and I got the offer from most of the companies with a significant raise in salary and a good position, but still, there were only four job changes in my thirty-year career.

If you asked me whether I am satisfied with my current level of career achievement, then I would say no, I am not.

Then why have I only changed a few jobs? Once again, the cycle of good

Luck and bad Luck played a vital role in opting for a new opportunity, which is why this funny book existed.

The story was different; we could not talk to you through this book.

Destiny wanted me to connect with millions of people and spread their love and affection with everyone through this book.

I often mentioned in this book that you can't decide your destiny as it is already there, and you are just a theater actor who plays a role and disappears from the stage once it is over.

I refused or not got the offer of many jobs not because of money, location, or position; there was only a common reason; you might laugh or feel sad that it was nothing but a last-minute change in my new job profile, which isn't funny.

Yes, it was fun for those employers, but it was a great management lesson for me that you should only be relaxed and complacent once you have finished your task, and you can't predict last-minute planning changes in your mind.

I want to share a few such incidents where I got a whole platter of food to eat, and later, in the last moment, when I was ready to have a meal, the platter was taken away just before my finger touched the dish.

I got an opportunity to interview from a well-reputed chemical company for the position of plant head; it was a very honorable, handsome opportunity for me.

Per the fixed schedule, I reached for the interview on a beautiful day.

It lasted for around three hours; I could satisfy the interview panel by answering all their questions.

Finally, the company chairman interviewed me. We all know the last interview with the chairman was only a formality.

Chairman also cleared me and congratulated me for the new assignment with their company and association for a long-lasting relationship as a formal gesture.

I had asked to wait half an hour for the offer letter formalities.

After half an hour, one of the company directors called me for further discussion.

My excitement was on the highest level because I was getting my dream job with an excellent salary package and how. I decided not to share this news with my family.

Good Luck was smiling; now he had complete confidence in my capabilities.

I entered the director's office, and with a pleasing smile, he welcomed me again and requested to sit.

I could not control the level of happiness within me; in a very short time, I would share this good news with my family, but I was not aware that this was the silence before the Tsunami that would rattle my dream once again.

He once again went through my resume and held himself at one point and asked that you have excellent exposure to EHS, i.e., Environment, Health, and safety; that is an additional experience with you; now we are thinking differently; we would like to offer you an EHS head position with same salary and designation of a general manager instead offering you a unit head position, now tell us are you ready to accept this changed offer.

I did not expect to face this unfortunate tricky situation.

As a chemical engineer by qualification, dreaming of a plant head job in the chemical industry is everyone's wish.

This wish lasted only half an hour; I had only very few seconds to respond to him.

Sometimes your inner voice is the best judge and also the best friend to help you make the correct decision.

My conscience immediately told me not to compromise and not to accept the revised offer; he told me it is the character of the company that they have shown in a very short period means you can't trust such an organization that can't sustain their decision and changes so instantly so I should not accept their terms and conditions.

After the final exchange of greetings, I immediately told them no and left the organization for my original destination.

I could compromise and accept the offer, but this would not be wise.

Destiny had a different plan for me; after two years, I learned that the company had stopped production and was bankrupt due to some financial fraud by management.

Bad Luck again converted into good Luck. It was a razor-shaven escape.

My only request to every reader of this book is to continually thank God for whatever you currently have.

He is very kind to everyone and always helps to fulfill your wishes sooner or later.

One more funny incident would like to share with you. It was astonishing and unbelievable to me.

You should earn the blessing of everyone; this blessing account balance sheet should always be positive, which means full of credit; later on, one day, you will get this back, but on the other side of the coin, your bad doing of past about that you may not be aware plays its role to discredit you earned credit.

As usual, on a beautiful day, when I was busy at my current job, I got a call from one of a potential employer who was supposed to be my company's existing customer too.

It was a big MNC, and the opportunity was significant; it was a country quality and technical head position for a club of around ten units.

It was a big responsibility, a challenging task, and a once-in-a-lifetime opportunity I received through a job consultant.

An interview panel comprised of all field experts of five people interviewed me for more than two hours.

One of the luckiest people on this earth passed the litmus test and was selected; it was another happiest moment for me.

The next day, I got a call from HR to finalize the salary and position; everything was in line; they asked to arrange my current salary detail and other supporting documents that I had placed.

I got communication that in a couple of days, they are sending the final offer letter to me, and I'd given my joining date to them.

I had to wait for a few days with a couple of follow-ups.

They informed me that due to their preoccupation with another position interview, it is getting a slight delay.

Days turned into weeks, and hope turned into sadness.

Later, I learned that the company was short of funds to accommodate this new position, and they decided to manage this requirement with their existing setup.

Once again, my bad Luck won over good Luck.

This time bad Luck was once again laughing at me, dancing joyfully, and making fun of good Luck.

Good Luck was feeling harassed and saw towards me and told me that tough times never last long, but arduous people last long, so don't bother about this lousy weather; blue sky with the shining bright sun is waiting for you.

Good Luck gave another motivational speech; such motivation gives you the strength to go ahead and never see behind.

Past experiences are a lesson to prepare for the betterment of the future ahead.

One more incident would like to share with you when I was on an official trip to South Africa, that time I was looking for a change.

I was in Durban, a magnificent green-lustered city with a beautiful seashore for the sea sport.

I'd stayed there for a month, and the place was beside the significant golf ground.

In the morning, beautiful deer used to visit there. It was a beautiful scenery place to stay there.

Good Luck came to me on a charming and beautiful morning and, with an initial greeting, informed me that today an opportunity would knock on your door. Be ready.

That time I was having a cup of tea offered by a sober, mature kitchen attendant. In South Africa, people always offer you a full big tea cup instead of a tiny Indian tea cup.

Once again, the stage was ready for the new play. The actor was the same, but the content was different.

I was the center of attraction. This time opportunity was for Indonesia, and it was a very senior position: new country, new culture, new language, new people, and new work environment.

What help else can you get from Good Luck?

What best he could have offered to me, he did.

Now it was my turn. Once again, I'd played my role very well; in the interview panel, most members were my old senior colleagues.

A tough interview session lasted for almost an hour.

My knowledge won their hearts.

I won, and they declared me a winner; what else can you get now? Bad Luck was waiting for his chance and planning how to spoil the show.

This time I was confident that my past good doing would help me, and the almighty will bless me.

Still, I was unaware of my hidden old debt account that had been pending payment for years, and the time arrived to pack back those debts with compounding interest.

Suddenly, all those good-hearted people disappeared from the scene.

Everyone became silent. There was a pin-drop silence from the interview panel, no response; I was crying; bad Luck once again had a bigger laugh, but surprisingly good Luck this time was not harassed but had a bigger laugh than bad Luck.

The smile of bad Luck vanished in a very short week because my different job change story had already begun.

I immediately got another excellent opportunity and finally got selected within fifteen days, changing my professional and personal life in all aspects.

I learned a lot of many life lessons before I left the organization, which are mandatory to survive in this harsh, throat-cut, competitive world.

I am thankful to all for creating challenging situations for me to stay,

Once again, a new journey with new hope at a new destination started searching for a new funny story with power wrestling of Good and Bad Luck.

The Moral of a Story

"Throughout the year, the weather gets changes and always follows a fixed cycle that no one can change. It is the rule of the universe. You have only to follow the same. Everything is already there on a blackboard in black and white; no one can change it; if someone thinks he is making the change, he is by mistake. Forget it, and remember, you are only the executor.

So be happy and enjoy your life with whatever you have, because whatever you have taken from here only and whatever you have given to here only. You came here empty-handed and will go back empty-handed".

Chapter 17

First ATR Flight > Control or Loss of Control

"When everything seems to be going against you, remember that airplane takes off against the wind, not along the wind."
Henry Ford

Courtesy: First ATR Flight: Image for representation only
You might be thinking, what's new in this?

Millions of people travel around the world, and such things are part of travel; you have to go through this; there is nothing special in this, and you may skip this chapter, but I request that you go through and enjoy and predict the unpredictable.

Sometimes funny things happen when you think it is the last day of your life and suddenly you find, oh no, it is not, and you are surprised how this happened.

I want to share one incident of air travel.

It was not my first travel, and as usual, I was at the airport for my routine journey to my destination (My home town) after finishing my everyday official work; there was nothing special there.

But something special was there; it was my first traveling by ATR flight; it is a small plane with limited passenger capacity, and the aircraft's speed is about half that of the Boeing aircraft.

My three more colleagues were traveling with me; a couple of them were coming for the first time touring the air, and it was the first opportunity for them, so it was an exciting moment for them.

They had never seen our beautiful earth from the sky and especially when you are traveling by evening flight when there is a time of sunset and night was spreading its beautiful wings to cover the earth.

At the same time, it was shining too with colorful lights like earth wore all the beautiful gold and diamond ornaments.

It was a pleasant scene visible from the window.

We served a delicious snack, and they enjoyed it a lot.

Everything was ok for the first half an hour. It was around two hours traveling to cover approximately 400 aeronautical miles.

Suspense and thriller were about to come, waiting for its time to show its importance to everyone.

Right now, fun was superseding both above. It was always a pleasant experience traveling with your friends.

If it is a twelve-hour journey, you will never realize when you reached your destination, and this was a short journey, so you had to enjoy every moment.

In life, you can't imagine consistency on the better side; deviation, or you can say variation, will be there.

Just after half an hour, trouble started, and no one was expecting this as it was a transparent cloud and good weather.

Suddenly big black cloud, which we could see through the window, started capturing the plane from all around.

It seemed that it would take our plane in its arms. Beautiful outdoor scenery turned into black darkness.

ATR is a tiny plane that may easily be turbulent by rough weather. Now skilled and experienced pilots can only run the plane through this odd.

Suddenly, turbulence started, the plane was vibrating, and slowly vibration became more and more severe.

I traveled regularly but never experienced such vibration as in a big jumbo plane.

You rarely feel such turbulence; this might be due to better aerodynamic balancing.

All around inside the plane, there was a moment of anxiety; people firmly held their chairs and started praying.

My all first-time air-traveling friend started crying and asking me what would happen now.

I was also scared but trying to calm down, that this was part of traveling and nothing will happen.

When you still have to cover 75 % of your journey and have no option but to remain seated, you can imagine the ultimate time to remember all your loved ones and recall all the bad and good things you have done in your whole life.

You apologize for your wrongdoings and promise God not to repeat the same if you survive.

Those few minutes are sufficient to see the complete picture of your life with all sorrow and happiness.

I can't explain in the word the climax of the scary moment that continued for more than an hour.

The heart was about to come out; blood pressure was at its peak, and people were hardly breathing.

In this situation, you are not in contact with the rest of the world except for the connectivity of the plane with ATC (Air Traffic Control).

It was the only positive sign of relief.

Can you imagine what would be the level of pressure on those twin pilots and crew?

The plane ran like an old car on a stony path with complete turbulence.

I'd never seen such a scene in my earlier and later air traveling. That was a real threatening moment.

At last, things started normalizing, and vibration came down drastically, and for a moment, there seemed to be pin-drop silence except for plane noise.

It remained for fifteen minutes, and we were about to land at our final destination.

The weather was once again pleasant.

Could you think of anything unexpected in the balance short time?

My friend, this is life, and it is tough to predict what is next.

Crew members and the pilots prepared to land in the next 15 minutes.

To our surprise, the sudden plane lost its control; in a normal landing, altitude gets reduced slightly, but this time plane started to go down freely; I don't know how much it was a height drop; it seemed about to crash within a minute.

This time everyone was shouting and crying loudly.

I was also one of them, as we had not expected.

I thought, now it's over, it is the final journey, and we will be the big story on tomorrow's newspaper and news channels.

I remembered this was the last time to say goodbye to all my family members with tears.

Bad luck was once again smiling on his win but also very sad because he never expected such a short closure of this life story; in fact, he did not like this.

You might be thinking then, how did I write this book, and currently, you are reading this with a climax that what will happen next?

Miracle happened!!!

All of those skilled pilots, whom I thought were very brave, and in situations even, they could also lose their lives.

Suddenly, both pilots got control of the plane when it was shortly about to touch the ground by writing a history for all of us; it again reached the continual altitude and finally stabilized.

Everyone was silent; it was fear or happiness, I don't know, but it was sure that the second inning of life commenced again.

Finally, we safely touched the ground.

Good luck won the race again, but bad luck was also smiling this time as a game of life of win and loss started again like a comic cartoon character, Tom & Jerry.

How did you like this battle between life and death?

The Moral of a Story

"You have to die only once in your current life; you can't repeat even twice. If this is to happen only once, then why worry about death? Enjoy your life to the best possible extent, and spread love and affection in your environment. Be happy, keep everyone happy, and enjoy".

Chapter 18

My Job Change Interview > Whether God Is Everywhere?

"The only way to do great work is to love what you do. If you haven't found it yet, keep looking. Don't settle".
Steve Jobs

Courtesy: Job change: Image for representation only

Our body comprises five essential elements, e.g., Water, fire, air, earth, and sun. It is not my new modern theory but an ancient one.

New modern science is also approved this.

Every matter consists of trillions of tiny molecules, and some force or energy bounds them.

One drop of Water consists of millions of molecules of hydrogen and oxygen.

We all believe in god and pray in different forms to get the blessing.

All over the world, in some form, we worship our god.

Everyone prays to get rid of bad happening and wishes for good fortune for them.

If we have such a belief, can we say that god is omnipresent in every particle of this universe?

Sometimes we do surprise that something good or bad happens to any individual without their knowledge.

Many times we see people survive any near-missed accident, and thousands of videos on YouTube are available to witness the same.

You might think this book is supposed to be fun and related to good or bad Luck, but here it is the storytelling about spirituality with mixed funny good and bad Luck.

We need to find out how many galaxies there are, how many lives there are in this universe, and who the super intellectual computer power is managing decillions of tiny pieces of information with so much accuracy without any error.

In statistical analysis, it is more than six sigma; it could be a hundred or more.

Six sigma is a helpful tool to measure the system's accuracy with minimum deviation from the standard: highest accuracy, the highest sigma level.

We don't have tools to measure the accuracy of the act of god's work.

No one can challenge him. You have to accept his all conduct and blessing with grace.

Whatever I told her, I felt the indirect presence of him through his act played by different actors at different points in time.

It is one of the experiences I am sharing with you that was full of thriller and suspense till the climax.

I was looking for a job change and started looking with competitor companies for better prospects, positions, and good salaries.

I got the opportunity with one of the companies for a job interview.

HR fixed the interview date.

I had to be interviewed by top management.

I had to travel more than four hundred kilometers from my residence to the destination.

I had the only option to reach there by bus only.

I had to reach there before noon as the interview panel was leaving the site at around 2 PM to catch the flight to their head office.

I told them it was ok with me and I shall be there by 8 AM because it was hardly an eight hours' journey.

If I start by 10 in the evening day before, I will reach there early in the morning by 6 AM, well six hours before the inter-view time.

Based on my earlier traveling experience, I'd pick up the last bus from my residence; it was very convenient for me.

Bus left for a destination on a scheduled time.

The journey was very smooth for the first one and a half hours.

I was enjoying classical music and sometimes chatting with close friends and getting some interview tips; although I'd appeared multiple times for the interview, this time, I was looking for a job change in my hometown.

There is a saying you enjoy your better present but always be ready for the worst.

This time I needed to prepare for the surprise that was about to touch me in a few moments.

Problems never tell you in advance of their arrival. The same happened to me; the good-running bus had suddenly broken down.

We all travelers thought this was a minor issue and that the bus driver and his assistant would handle it.

We all waited for the fixing of the problem, but we could not realize that situation would be more complicated shortly, and that would be the biggest surprise for me.

During the journey, the bus passed from a hilly area of a narrow-width road formed by cutting curved hills.

It was my first misfortunate; this bus got under break down at the start of the hilly area.

I had gathered information from the bus driver that this last bus used to go under breakdown frequently due to poor maintenance by the bus owner.

This time problem arises wasn't short-lived.

Driver, after an hour, declared that he immediately could not fix the problem, there was a need for repairing some machine parts, and he didn't have spares.

Either it had to repair or arrange. The replacement; Time was 1 AM, and we were at a height of around two thousand feet.

The first good Luck was a full moon day, so moonlight relieved us.

But adversity was coming one by one; it was the pick winter season, the temperature was around 3~4 degree Celsius, and chilled air was repeatedly striking my bus.

We had no option but to wait as no other bus from any travel agency followed; I was traveling by the last bus.

Shortly after I'd come down and enquired nearby, I got little relief that this bus got tripped near the police toll check.

A few policemen were managing the traffic and sitting around the campfire.

I reached out to them to maintain the body temperature.

There is also a saying that an evil time continually tests you; another lousy news that reached me was a heavy traffic jam due to the breakdown of one commercial vehicle on the way, someone kilometer ahead of my bus.

There was no chance of getting of mess clear by the morning.

I was shocked now; reaching before noon was very difficult.

In the meantime, one policeman offered me a cup of tea; it was a delightful surprise; it is rarely happening that they were so polite with me.

Generally, in my last half an hour observation to ensure smooth traffic management, they were very tough with bus, truck, and lorry drivers.

When I again enquired about the bus, his assistant said the driver went out to repair the damaged part, but he was still determining when he would return due to jamming.

I requested one policeman to use their authority to instruct the lorry driver to carry me and at least drop me at the next station, the national highway.

From there, I could catch the other bus and reach on time.

They promised me, it would be another pleasant moment for me at that time.

They told me that they would find an appropriate vehicle for me.

Time passed slowly; it was 3 AM at night, and I was not relieved.

I'd once again requested them if there was any other bus from any other place If coming on this route, please tell them to drop me till the next station as traffic was in a hilly area only. They promised me.

I had to wait for one more hour on a chilly night, my heartbeats were rising, and I was helpless, the poor guy with no clue what to do next.

Meanwhile, I've tried several lorry drivers, but they did not respond positively.

At 4 AM, I prayed the god and finally decided to sit on the bus to get some sleep because I could not sleep for a moment on the chilled night.

You might know that time between 3 AM to 5 AM is the golden time of the day; during this period, all the universe's power bestows its blessing on their loved one, this was my belief, and this has been happening for thousands of years.

It was the golden opportunity for me, for which I had been working from last month, and this slowly started slipping from my hands.

A miracle happened suddenly; I could not believe this could be possible.

As soon as I entered the bus and was about to sit, a luxury bus from another location came, and that bus driver stopped his bus parallel to my bus.

He asked me, where do you want to go? Come immediately on our bus, and we will drop you at the next station.

Oh my god, you are everywhere; no one can challenge you, only get his blessing.

I immediately shifted to that bus, and suddenly, traffic congestion that lasted four hours got cleared.

I thanked god and sit on the bus. It might be those policemen whom I had requested many times informed this bus driver to catch me.

I'd reached the next station by 6 AM; now I had only six hours to go there.

I feel like the luckiest person on earth again.

But, But ....

Challenges still needed to be ended.

I had been dropped off at the highway by this bus.

From my basic understanding, I could catch another bus to reach the destination.

My assumption was wrong; no single bus from that route was passing that route in the next hour.

Now it was 7 AM, and I had to travel a distance of around 200 more kilometers to reach there.

To my shocked surprise, that was different from the bus route, and I had to reach a bus station around five kilometers from that place to catch the correct bus.

I caught the taxi and reached there, it was already 8 AM, time was getting shorter and shorter now, and the first bus from that place was about to start at 9 AM only, I had to wait till this time.

Now it was almost impossible to reach there. I had communicated to the

HR person that it would be challenging for me to be on time. He only told me how to contact him before leaving the interview panel.

Finally, the bus started on time, or with the precise scheduled time precisely at 9 AM as per schedule.

Another journey started, and a helpless guy like me began to pray once again to give the bus driver some additional sense of urgency.

There is power in the prayer; if you do it with a true heart, the whole universe begins to work for you to fulfill your wish; it is a time and tested nature's tool that no one can deny.

My faithful pray started to work like a miracle, I never experienced in my earlier bus rides.

Suddenly, that old, experienced driver started pressing the accelerator of the bus; now, the wheels were moving at a rising speed, he was driving the bus like racing with a racecourse horse, and he had decided to win the race for me only.

In between the destination and the first station, there were around six towns, and everywhere as per my experience, the bus had to stop for a minimum of fifteen minutes each.

But to my surprise, he hardly stopped for a minute or two or didn't stop due to a lack of travelers or very few travelers.

Most passengers who boarded the bus were only for the last station.

I had to reach by noon, but even after the bullet speed of the bus, I could only arrive after 1 PM. Immediately I called

HR for my late arrival and requested to communicate with the interview panel accordingly.

I had to reach there within an hour as the interview panel was leaving the site to catch their flight; it was a question of someone's life and death.

To my relief, I got a communication from HR that they could wait for me.

The bus continuously moved, and I was just 25 kilometers from my company vehicle pickup point.

After that, I had to travel 30 more kilometers in the company vehicle to reach the final destination.

Suddenly, the bus driver stopped the bus for the next 30 minutes for lunch.

Oh shit! It was still pending to surprise me; now, no way I could; no other option was left. It was a big blow to me.

I had to wait for the following public transport vehicle and was curious when it would come.

I'd started getting repeated calls from HR and the company vehicle driver about my arrival. It was now 01:15 PM.

With all my frustration, I stood on the highway, kept my head down, and was just about to tear my eyes; another miracle happened; from another route, one superfast small passenger bus arrived and stopped in front of me.

A person operating the bus called me to come inside; it was like a grasping at straws.

That bus carried to pick a point in the next fifteen minutes at the fastest speed.

In all my journey, I'd never asked the driver to run the bus fast, it was just happening to me, and nature was pouring her love and smile over me.

At 01:30 PM, I reached the pickup point; the driver was waiting for me; his morning shift was about to finish by 2 PM.

Now the time gap has been reduced to 30 minutes only; the driver was aware of the urgency, and as per his communications during the travel, he told me that he was running the company car with the highest speed of more than 100~120 kilometers per hour against the maximum set limit of 80 kilometers per hour.

It was his highest career car speed, he claimed.

While traveling, I changed my clothes in the vehicle to prepare for the direct interview, even though I had not done my toothbrush.

Finally, by 2 PM, I entered the company, interview panel was waiting for me only.

In a general scenario, the interview typically lasts for two to three hours for a very senior position.

Good Luck was already present at reception there, and he welcomed me with a broad smile; due to a shortage of time, they interviewed me for only fifteen minutes, and after all satisfactory answers, I got the job.

Oh my god, I got it.

That never happened before; I hope this will not repeat, and it should not happen to anyone like this way.

My sixteen hours of miracle journey, full of suspense, thrillers, and climax, I finally ended with a pleasant outcome.

All is well when the end is well.

What do you say after reading the story? Is there anyone above us who takes care of every individual with so much meticulous planning and perfection? It is not an excellence but only a perfection.

Thank you a lot, oh almighty.

The Moral of a Story

"When odds obstruct the way of your target, do not lose your patience, be calm and cool. There are multiple ways to reach the final destination when there is a will. Believe in yourself and on almighty god".

Chapter 19

COVID-19 Lock Down> New Opportunity & Spiritual Journey

"Prepare a Motivational Speech during these Covid-19 times to tell the future generation the power of being optimistic".

Somya Kedia, A motivational speaker

Courtesy: Spiritual opportunity: Image for representation only

A Pandemic is a life-threatening infectious disease.

It had turned around the whole world by 360 degrees by changing the life of the people.

People started learning the new normal.

It drastically changed every individual's cultural, social, personal, and financial values.

Every kind of relationship took a new paradigm and forced individuals to adopt the same.

Brotherhood-ness was replaced with personalized priority there; everyone was looking after self-protection from any individual loss in all aspects.

Peoples were more worried and insecure—the concept of after you are replaced by before you.

It is the one side of the coin that is a darker shade of life, but the other side of the coin is brighter in appearance.

It is more promising and also changes the individual's life.

One phrase is the survival of the fittest. People started learning the new art of survival.

Hidden talent and creativity in idle time surfaced.

Self-dependency had replaced interdependency.

Multiskilling became the need of the hour and a mandatory requirement.

In such a situation, surviving would only be easy if you had other skills.

A hobby became a professional adventure and another source of earnings as no one knew how long this pandemic would have lasted.

I was also one of the victims of the lockdown. Although I was not affected financially much, this gave me ample opportunity to identify hidden talent within me.

It was a complete pleasant surprise to me. I had inferior writing skills; you might be thinking what great I had written at this stage, but my friend, I have miles to go.

Friends, to cover a long distance, you must take the first step and remain confident unless you achieve the objective that determination and persistence you have to show to yourself.

After a long industry experience in FMCG (Fast Moving Consumer Goods) industry and operational excellence, I'd compile this knowledge and convert it into a simple language readable from small articles and publish small blogs on my website.

Nothing will go to waste; each available piece on this earth has some value or usefulness in some way or another.

Before this pandemic, I had planned to do a digital marketing course; the idea was to develop my commercial website through which I could earn some money.

I was blank on this subject. Frankly, it was not my cup of tea.

There is a saying that you should only poke your nose everywhere once you are competent enough to handle the assigned task.

I had a different plan and decided to go riding on a new adventure or acquire new business skills; I'd attended a three-month digital marketing paid course and obtained the desired skill.

Now, I am a trained digital marketing person.

I started slowly working on developing my website without any technical support and finally created my website, www.excellence2fmcg.com, which deals with the FMCG industry. The website is still live.

We do not know the source of the pandemic, whether it is artificial or naturally generated, but it is a disaster for all human beings.

Life converted from ordinary to the new standard.

I'd published one blog on this subject also.

I'd take maximum advantage of the lockdown period.

After my working hours, I was independent as my family was in other places, and due to travel restrictions, it was impossible from either side to visit anyone and meet physically.

It was a golden opportunity bestowed by god to me to harness my digital marketing skill and my writing, English grammar, and presentation skills.

I learned many techniques and experimented with many permutations and combinations in designing my website, web pages, and blogs.

During this period, I also learned a new skill of writing digital books and publishing them on an online global platform.

This time you might be thinking that he is having good fortune and has ample time to spend on this.

Once again, good luck was smiling at me.

I was on a seventh sky and getting whatever I had planned. Things were going in my favor.

During this period, I wrote two books and published them online, "Excellence2fmcg, for all FMCG students and professionals" and "One-minute food manager for all world travelers who are food lovers."

My third book, which is currently in your hand, was also started during the lockdown period.

Many times I heard that you will get the return for your hard work.

There is no perfect definition of success, or there is no boundary of perfection.

I have complete faith in my spiritual power that with their grace, one day, all three books and my commercial website will be a blockbuster.

My time will come.

I believe in karma; the good fruitful results will follow you; you don't need to panic and wait for this.

In one complete year, god gave me another opportunity to start my spiritual journey, which was my longtime dream.

It was the right time selected by the almighty to see life differently as a spiritual person, and it kept me away from my family.

Thank god, no one can understand your magic; you are everywhere.

It was a long duration for more than a year. I have stayed alone due to my commercial obligation due to my job as well as due to the restrictions of corona pandemic.

Earlier, due to my family priorities, I'd hardly had time to spare myself on a spiritual journey.

During this period, I saw many online discourses on this subject and tried to learn the significance of the current and past life—the connectivity of present life with our past many lives.

It was excellent learning many concepts like the law of attraction, the impact of past life cosmic account on your current life, perfect fabrication of life of all living things in this universe, and very micro level or I can say excellent Nano or even more level life planning of each life, manifestation, etc.

One of the most important concepts I've learned through this spiritual journey is that we decide our next future life on our own based on our current cosmic account.

You may think it is joking, but you will only realize it when you practice it.

You can buy all luxury of your life with money; this pleasure would be for the time being or temporary.

The pleasure you feel after this journey is priceless.

Before this exercise, I'd used to get panic even with a minor issue that started directly impacting my health, and the doctor alerted me of symptoms of potential heart-related problems, blood pressure, and blood sugar issue soon.

Once I started practicing this, there was an enormous change; I felt relaxed and started thinking things differently, which helped me maintain good health without any issues.

I should close this chapter now. I hope you have enjoyed this discussion a lot.

The Moral of a Story

"Don't panic about adverse situations; convert this into an opportunity to improve yourself. You might not know when your whole life will take a turnaround. The law of attraction says, "What you wish, and if you repeatedly feel and behave that you have accomplished this, in due course of time as per your terms and condition, you get it."

Chapter 20

My Corona and Vaccination > Where Are the Computer Server

"You may not always have a comfortable life. And you will not always be able to solve all the world's problems simultaneously. But don't underestimate your impact because history has shown us that courage can be contagious, and hope can take on a life of its own".
Michelle Obama

Courtesy: Corona vaccination: Image for representation only

Corona was the most searched keyword in the internet world.

The whole population around the world spent most of their time getting as much information as possible to keep themselves safe from this biggest pandemic of the century.

It had not only destroyed the world economy but the lifestyle of the individual.

There is a vast difference between pre-corona and post-corona lifestyles.

Social balancing is disturbed.

Social gatherings for better relationship turns into social distancing. In the old days, before social media's arrival, there was social distancing by default due to limited sources for one-to-one interaction.

People need better transportation facilities to meet each other.

This pandemic had done a disaster; loved ones who left for their final journey couldn't allow their close friends and relatives to at least pay their last homage to them before their final trip.

They were directly sent from the hospital to the place for their final rituals.

It never happened in the history of humanity.

People closed themselves to the four walls of their houses. It was the first kind of experience for everyone.

I was also a witness to this unique situation.

I had taken all the precautions to protect myself from any miss happening to me.

An unfortunate thing happened to me that I was alone due to my job change, and no one was there to take care of me if I was affected by Corona.

My family was at another location more than four hundred kilometers from my residence.

The government had suspended all means of transport as a precautionary measure.

The whole world was in a very panic situation, with growing deaths. No one was sure about their well-being in the coming days.

Day by day, week by week, month by month, I passed through the first corona wave, and everything normalized after ten months.

During this period, I was away from my family and was in touch with them through voice or video calls.

I planned to shift my family to my home town where I'd got a new job.

There was a happiest moment everywhere because everyone was physically meeting each other after a long duration.

To date, everyone is safe by the grace of god. I was thinking and praying for him to keep this blessing forever.

Many pharmaceutical companies were working in parallel on developing the corona vaccine.

Finally, they declared that vaccines are now available across the world for adults of more than 45 years of age.

I found myself lucky that at the right time, I shall get vaccinated and will get rid of this deadly disease.

I got my chance after three months of declaration due to the priority to health Volunteers.

On a beautiful day, I felt like the luckiest person to reach the vaccination center with my wife.

As a gesture after greeting all and policy of ladies first, my wife got her first corona vaccination without any trouble.

After all the digital formalities, she immediately got a notification on her mobile number for confirmation of the same.

It was my turn; as usual, I entered the center carrying all supporting documents.

There was a digital registration formality before vaccination.

I was relaxing but excited, too, with little worry, as I knew that after the vaccination, there would be a fever for a day with other side effects and pain.

The data entry operator started entering my detail in the system; as soon as he pressed the final enter key for my final registration, the computer server went down, to my surprise.

Now data entry operator needed to be made aware of whether I was registered.

In the meantime, he restarted the computer but needed to remember the login password as he never faced this situation earlier; he needed to learn about the password.

He called upon the technical guy for support and to resolve the issue.

After a struggle of half an hour, he finally managed to start the computer.

I curiously asked whether everything was in place, and he said yes, now you can go for your first corona vaccination.

I asked him how shall I got the intimation; he said don't worry, everything is alright; you will shortly get the same.

I said, ok, thanks and came out from the center.

But hours of waiting turned into days and months, but I still needed the system-generated message.

I'd noted my vaccination date, and the next vaccination, per health department protocol, was scheduled after 42 days.

It was the testing time for everyone as the second corona wave exponentially started spreading all around the corner.

The government once again immediately implemented strict corona protocols.

Fortunately, this time my family was with me.

My wife and kids were highly frustrated with the first wave-long restrictions, but this time, they were relaxed as they were in their hometown, our residence, and supporting neighbors.

During this fun time, as it was the summer holidays for kids, there was no online class pressure on them.

Everyone enjoyed their life the what we used to do during my childhood, but the extent of amusement was less because that was a natural phenomenon, and the current one was a forced phenomenon.

Soon 42 days' barrier was about to finish, and my wife and I were excited to take the second jab and get fully protected from this virus.

On a beautiful day, we both reached the vaccination center; my other eligible colleagues were with me for the second vaccination dose.

In a short time, Doctor came to us with a big smile who was a medical officer also for that campus; usually, all doctors treat their patients with smiles to ease their worries about diseases.

We were with all our documents to share with the medical team.

The registration team checked my earlier vaccination record, and once again, surprise; oh my god, why is it my only time and again? Why it happens to me only?

You might be thinking, what is new to me, friends? Another bad luck was before me; the medical team told me that, as per the record, I did not take my vaccination, and now I have to take my first vaccination; I told them I had already taken it.

You have to once again the record.

She once rechecked, and this time there was a smile on her face, so on my face, now bad turn into good, she said as per record, you got your first vaccination; my goodness, what is this?

But, earlier medical personnel did not verify it; this time, it is verified and will be considered the first vaccine.

Now I was ready for the second vaccine; Once again, the stage became ready.

You might be saying now that everything is ok with me, but my friend's show was still going on; this was not the happy ending; a big climax was about to come.

Smiled Doctor came to us and announced that the government had declared a short while ago on the same day that the second vaccination had extended the next 42 days.

Guys, what would you say now?

Another bad luck surprise. What can I do now? I had to go back and wait for the next date.

It was the only climax; the super finish was yet to come.

As soon as I reached home, I felt feverish and a body ache.

Soon fever crossed 100 deg Celsius; whether it was a sign of Corona or whether it found a place in my body too, now I had to verify.

After a couple of days, my whole family started feeling the same; the next day, we reached the Corona testing center and were anxious 24 hrs after the sampling. What will be next?

If it is a positive report, what will our next action plan be, and how will it be managed? We had spent the whole day in anxiety.

The next day, we had to wait a whole day for the report, but there was no message on my mobile phone for positive or negative news.

In a typical process, system generated digital report appears on mobile, but this was not the case with me.

Due to a system error, test reports could not be generated; hence they could not inform us, and another day went to waste.

Is this type of surprise a part of my life?

Finally, the next day, we got the call from Municipal Corporation that we all were Corona positive.

How to react, enjoy, or cry? We all decided to face this challenge and enjoy this isolation period.

After the proper consultation with a doctor, we received his medicine advice schedule.

In such a situation, people get broken down and start feeling that everything is lost and anxious about the future.

We had taken this positively because this was the first time in our life we were living together for such a more extended period.

You will not believe it; this was the only golden period of our life; we had to live every moment of that period.

Our routine life got changed but was full of enjoyment.

We spent quality time at home chatting, playing games, working on exercise, and many more. It never happened before, and I hope it will not recur again.

God bestowed his love to all of us.

Should I close this story now? Yes, or no?

The Moral of a Story

"Life is full of happiness and sadness; we must learn the art of living in all the good and bad weather. Every phase of life is a new teacher to you with new experiences. As obedient students, we have to experience this new learning to experiment in the future for the betterment of ourselves to become more refined".

And life is going on with many funny stories————————————————-

Epilogue

My lovely dear friends and passionate readers,

I am highly grateful to you for spending a perfect quality time reading this one unique book on altogether different kinds of genres right from the beginning till the end.

I hope this was an excellent experience for you.

I captured various dimensions of life at different life stages and tried to see them from different angles.

We see everything in this world very simply, but to understand each, you should have different glasses to this highly complex world.

Throughout this book's writing, I have touched on philosophy, science, technology, human values, family bonding, spirituality, the power of a superpower, and old and modern management principles and techniques.

I tried to experiment with all the above tools and techniques to evaluate suitability and effectiveness in a given situation.

It was an effort to say a lot with a few words.

This book could be a better composition of complicated grammar, unheard phrases, and English words.

I explained all concepts in a familiar, easy-to-understand layman's language for my global reader.

As I mentioned many times in this book, you often reach excellence in the journey of perfection.

This book is one kind of endeavor.

I will wait for your valuable feedback to make this book more exciting and shall be back with more interesting stories that, due to some constraints, couldn't become part of this first edition, but, in a short duration, this would be part of the second edition.

Thanks a lot.

I am reachable at my Email: manish260470@gmail.com

Don't miss out!

Visit the website below and you can sign up to receive emails whenever Manish Sharma publishes a new book. There's no charge and no obligation.

https://books2read.com/r/B-A-IZTZ-ITHMC

About the Author

A seasoned chemical engineer with Master of Science from BITS Pilani. A Certified Six sigma Black belt.

CQI & IRCA qualified lead auditor for ISO QMS 9001, 14001, 45001, and FSSC 22000, IMS (Integrated Management System).

Diploma from IIP (Indian Institute of Packaging), Mumbai

A Competent professional with over three decades of industry experience in Flexible packaging, Labeling, Lamination, Chemical Production, Product Development, Project Management, Customer Relationship, Quality Assurance, and Technical services.

Skilled in implementation of lean methodologies and 5S technique;

Hold competency in food packaging grade product legal and statutory compliance.

And last but not the least the spiritual practitioner, who believes that life journey is always a path of new experience for betterment.

Read more at https://excellence2fmcg.com/.

9 798223 132677